"Nature alone is antique,
and the oldest
art a mushroom."

— Thomas Carlyle

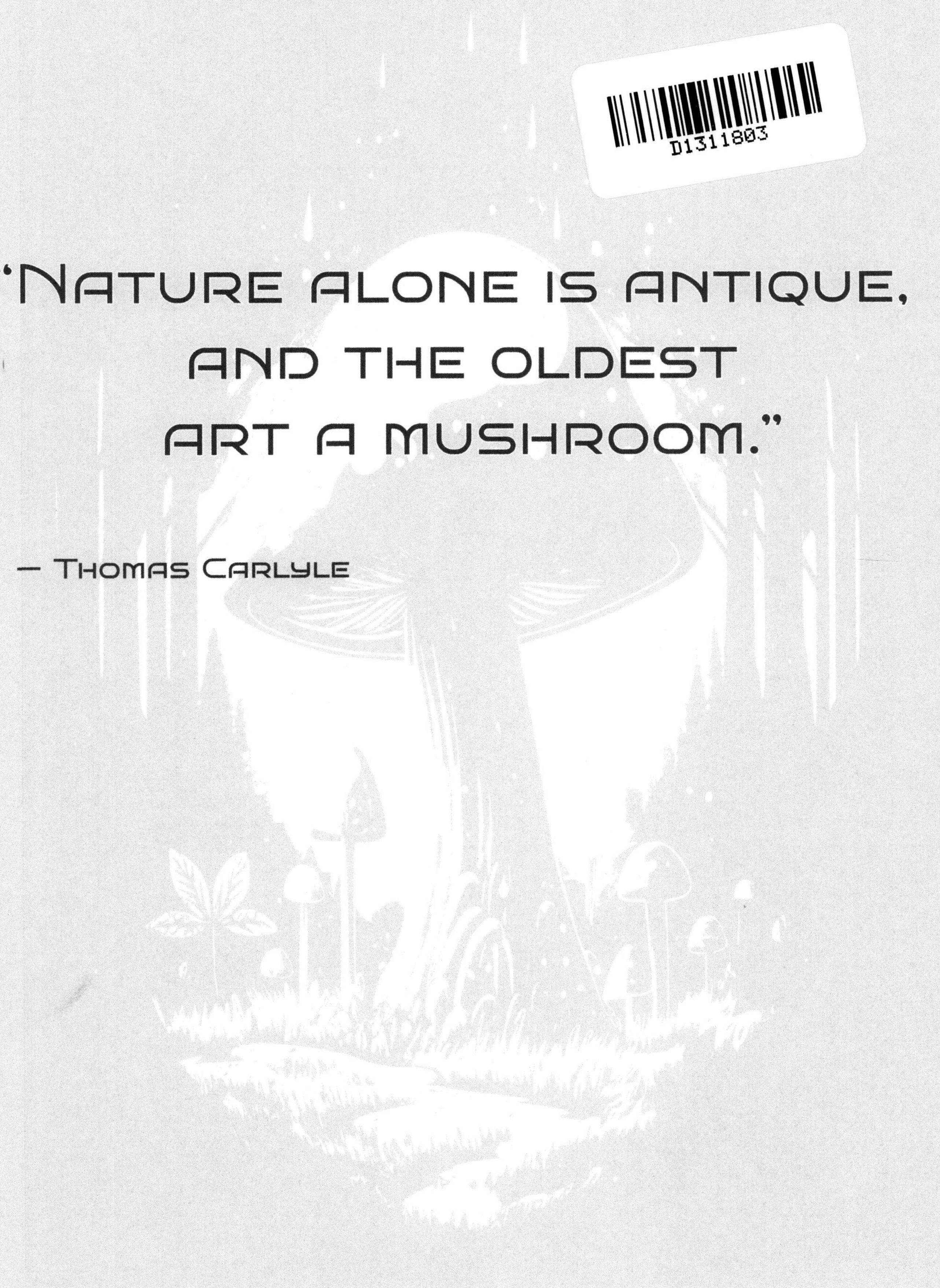

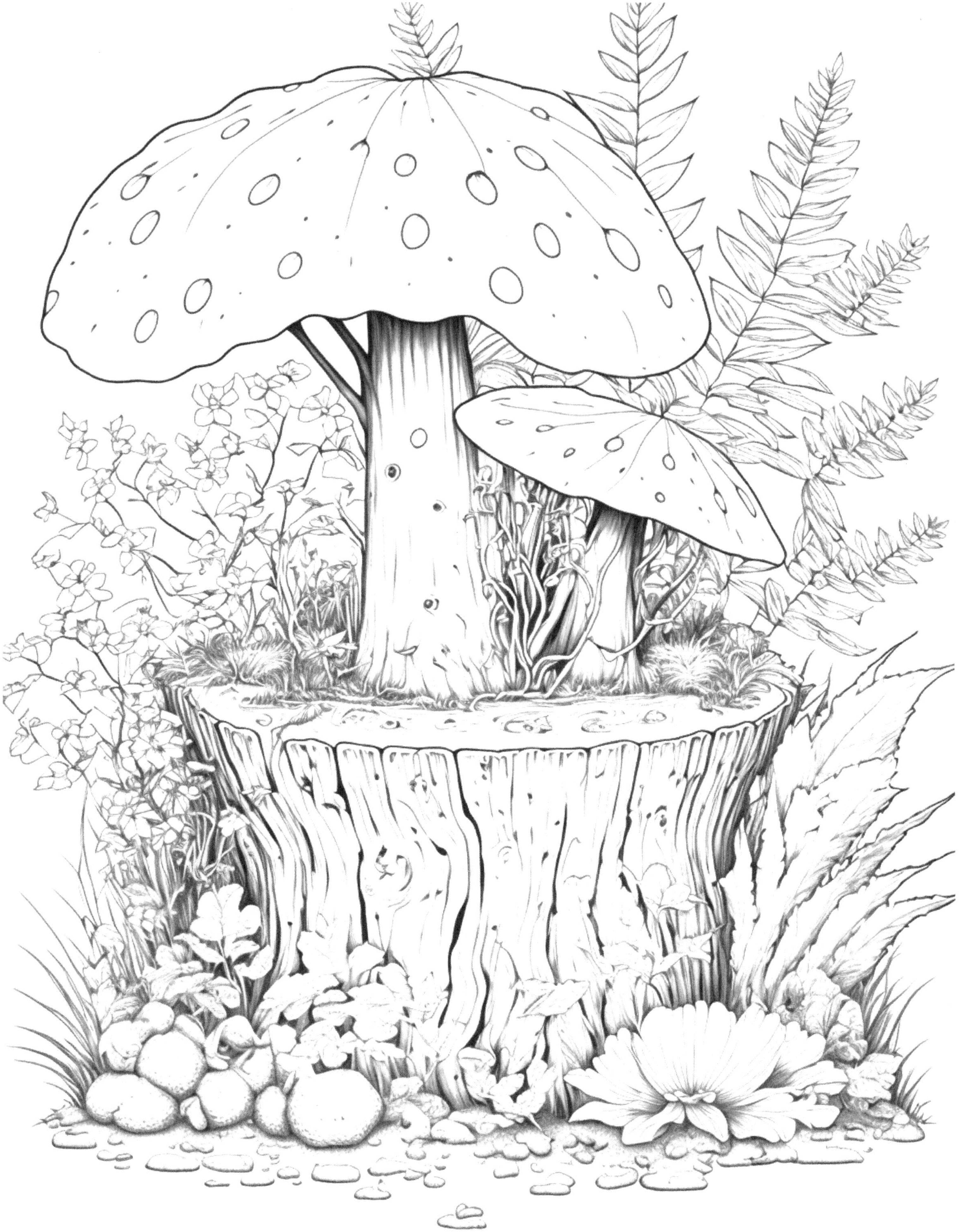

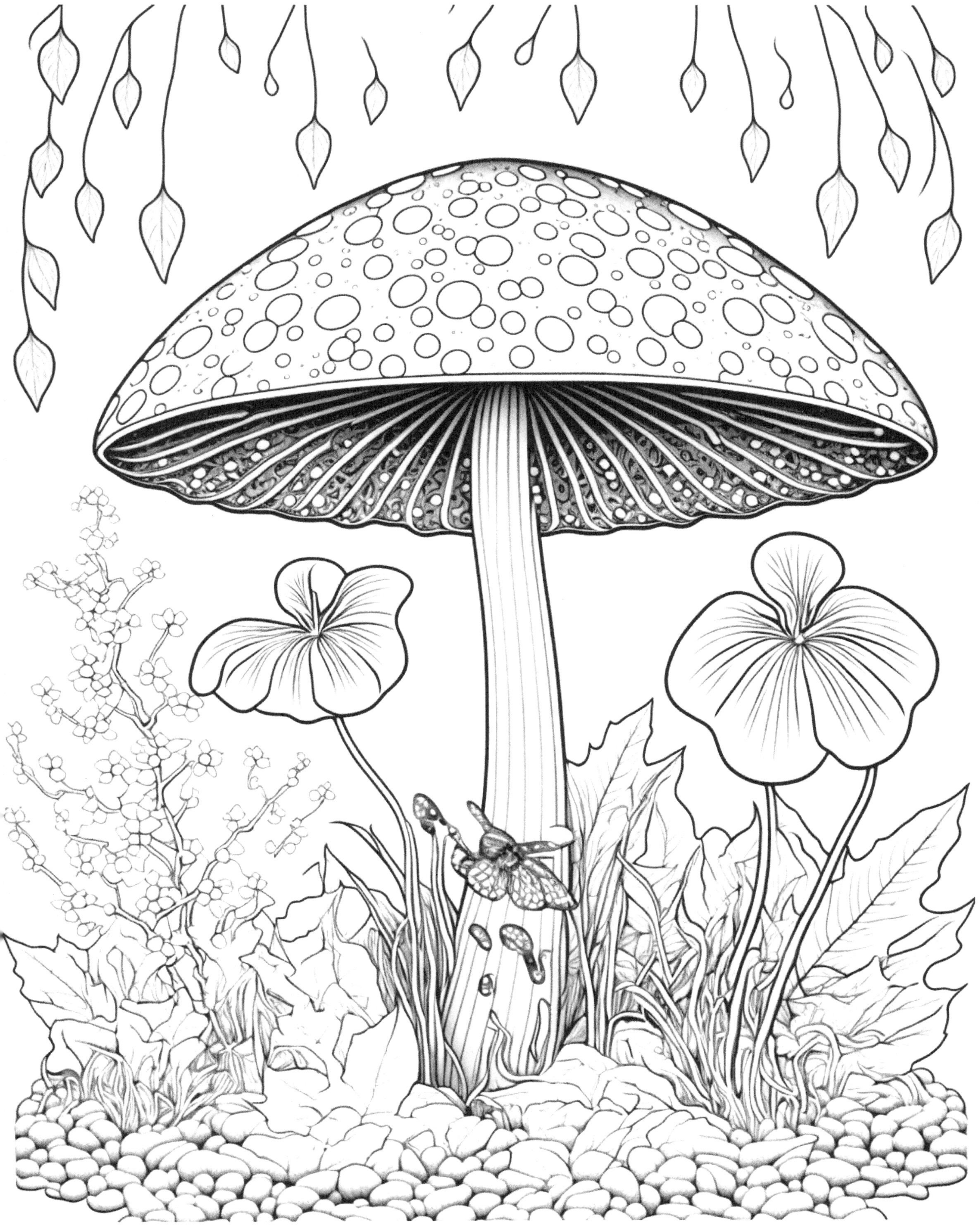

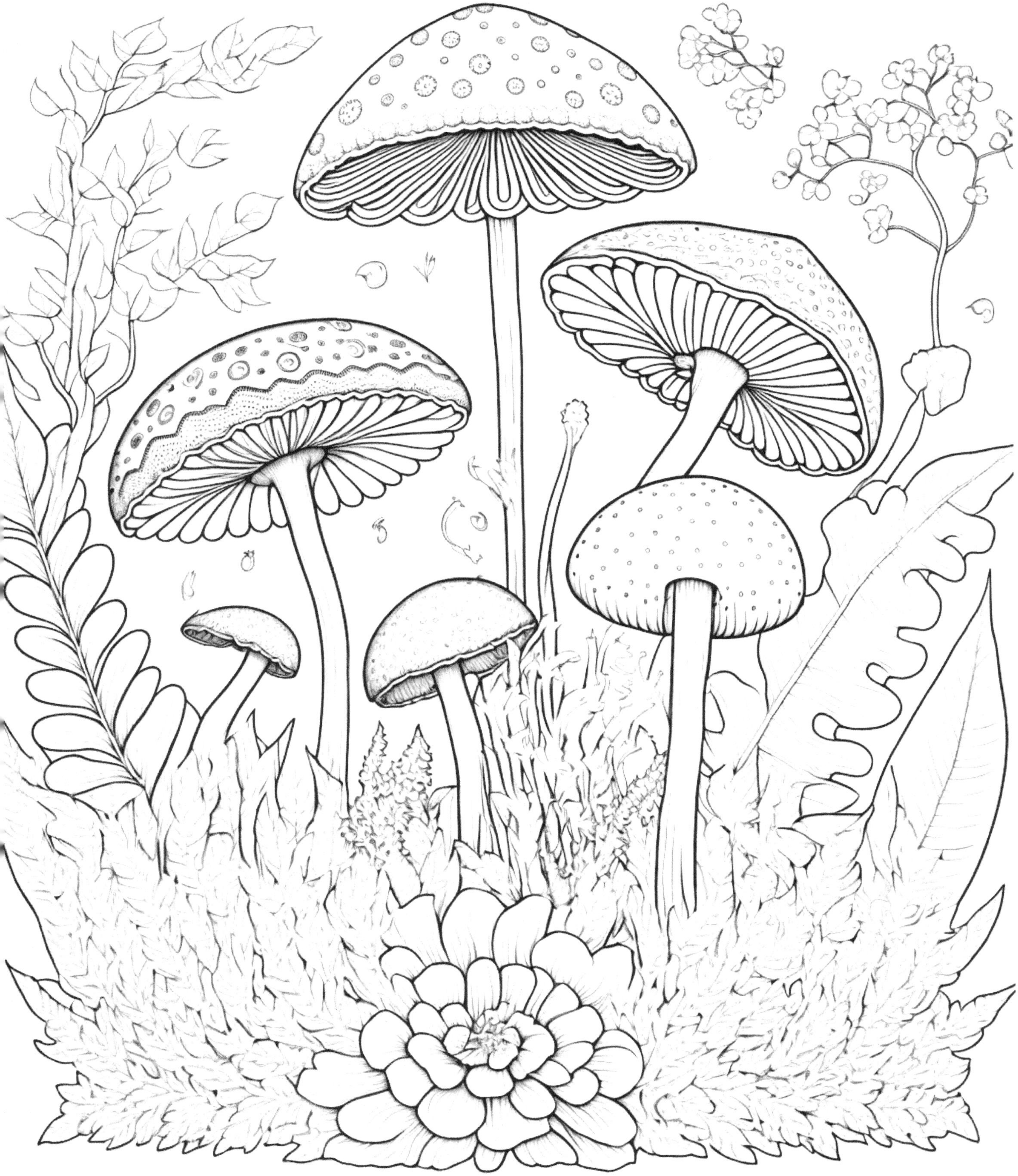

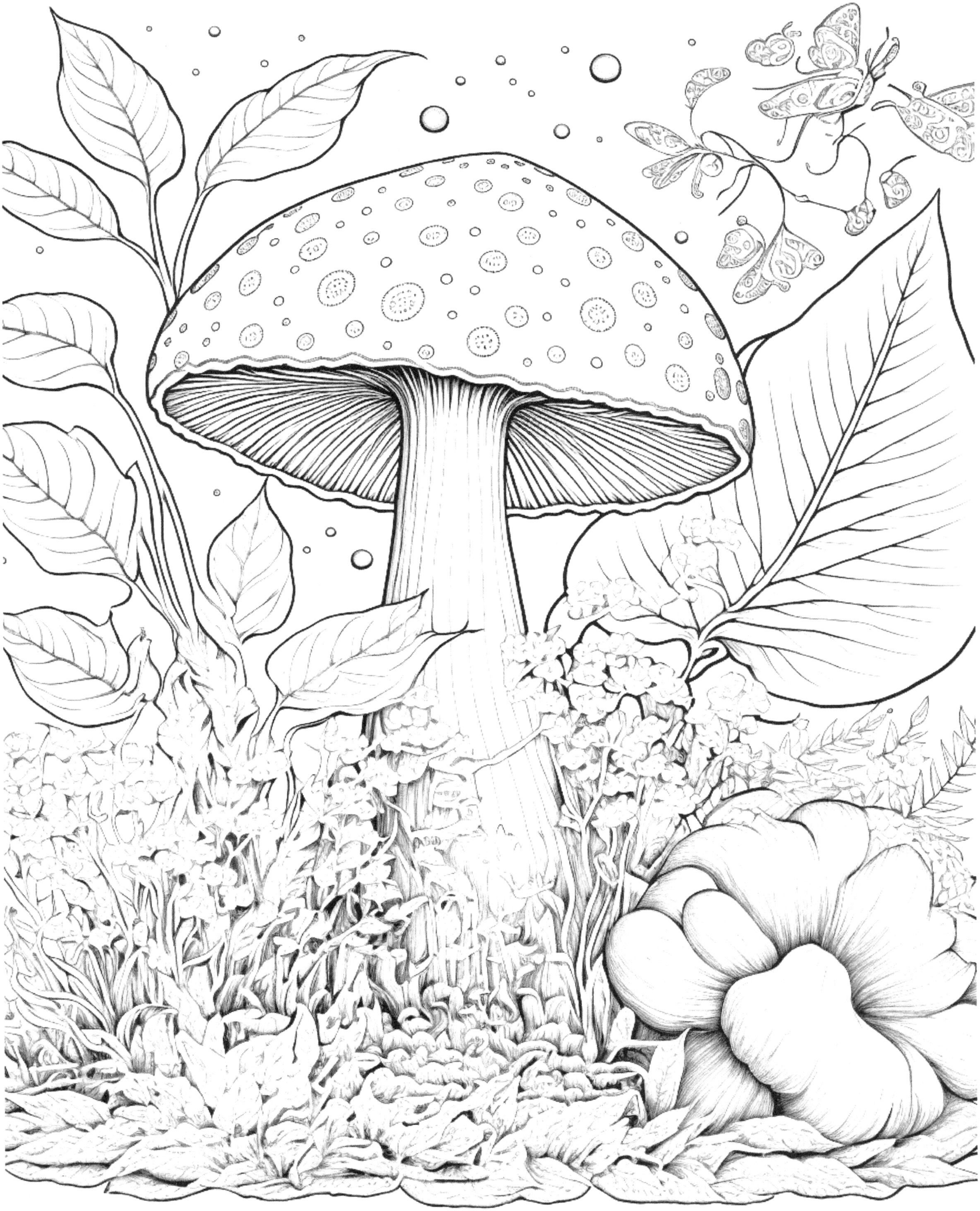

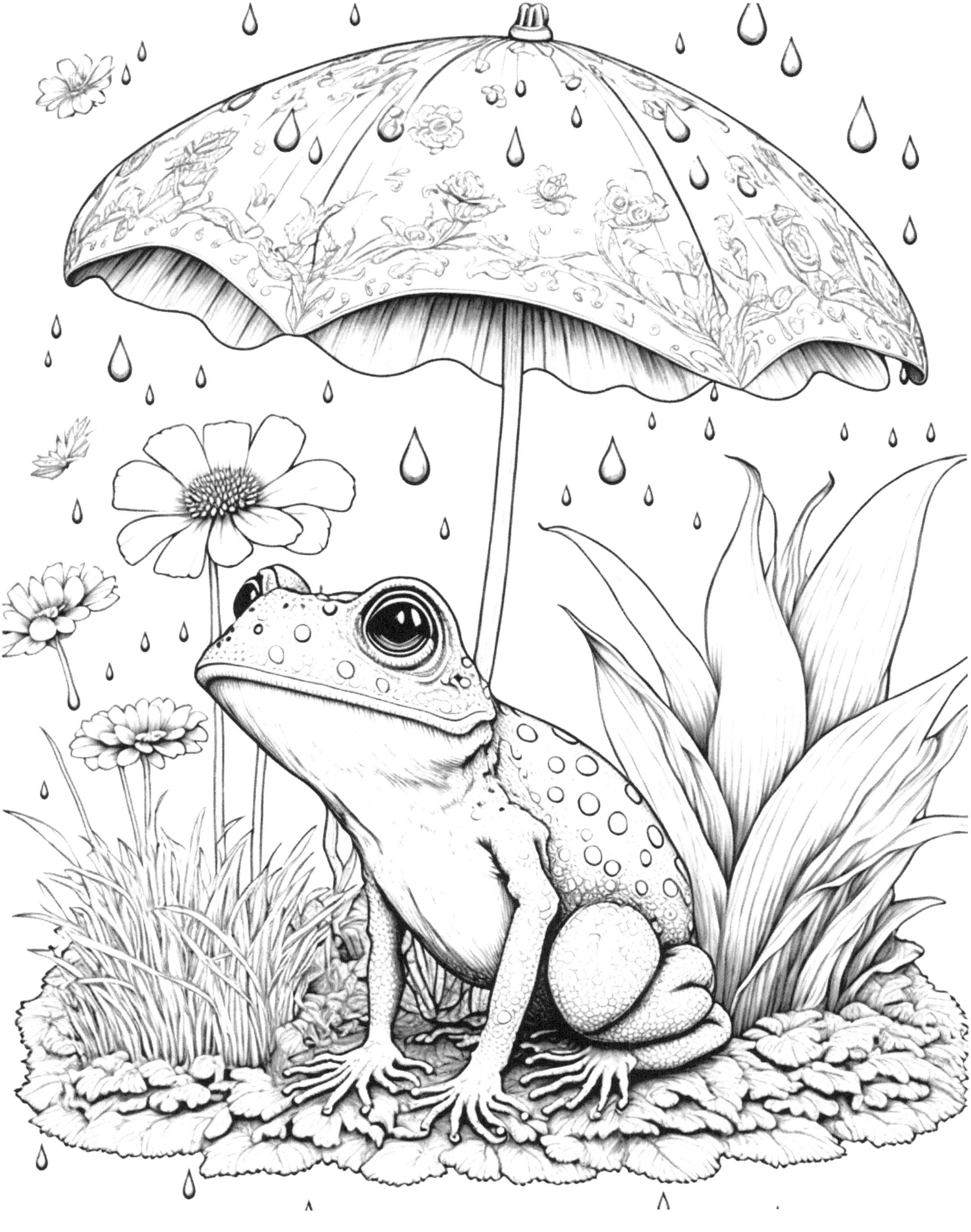

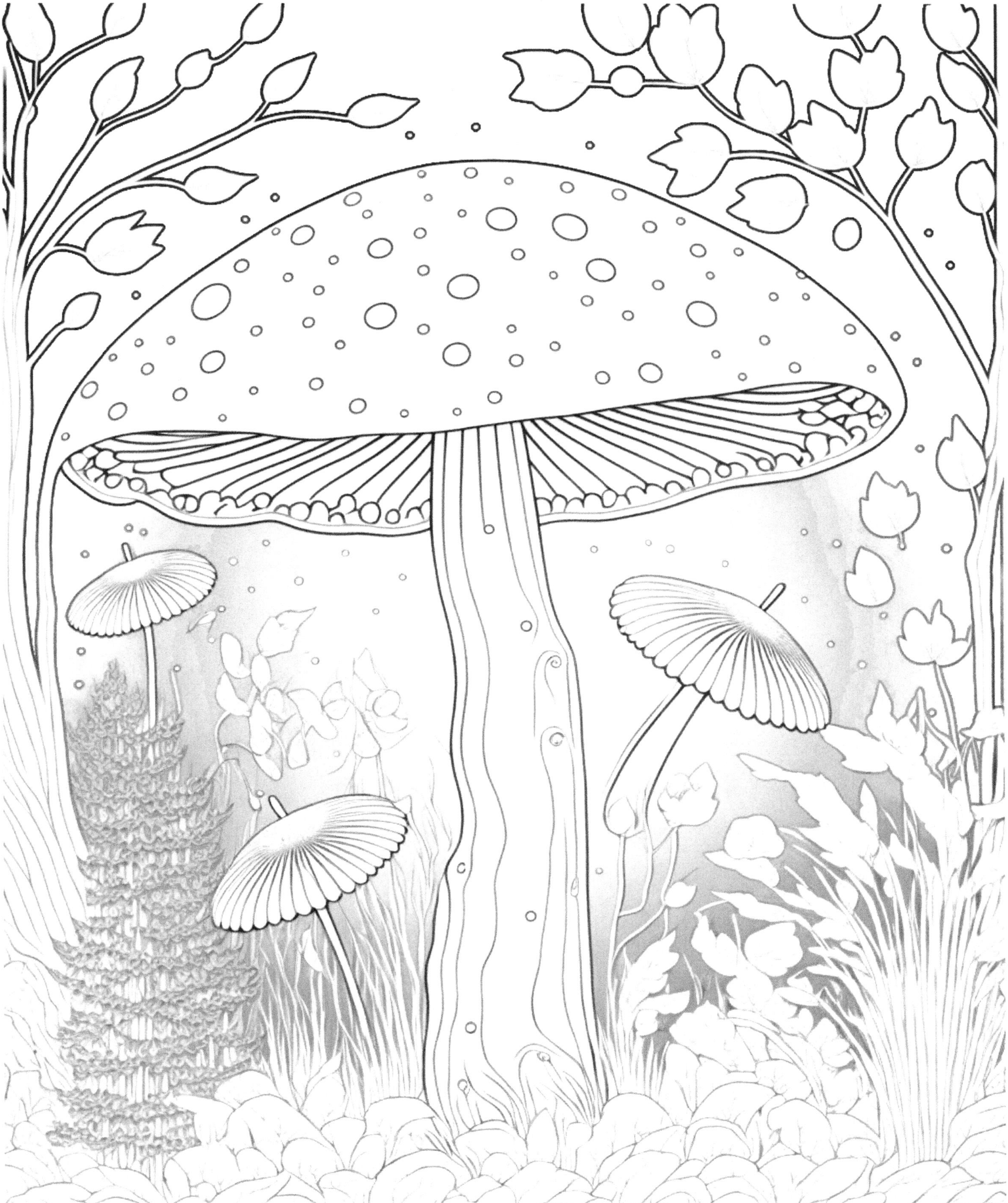

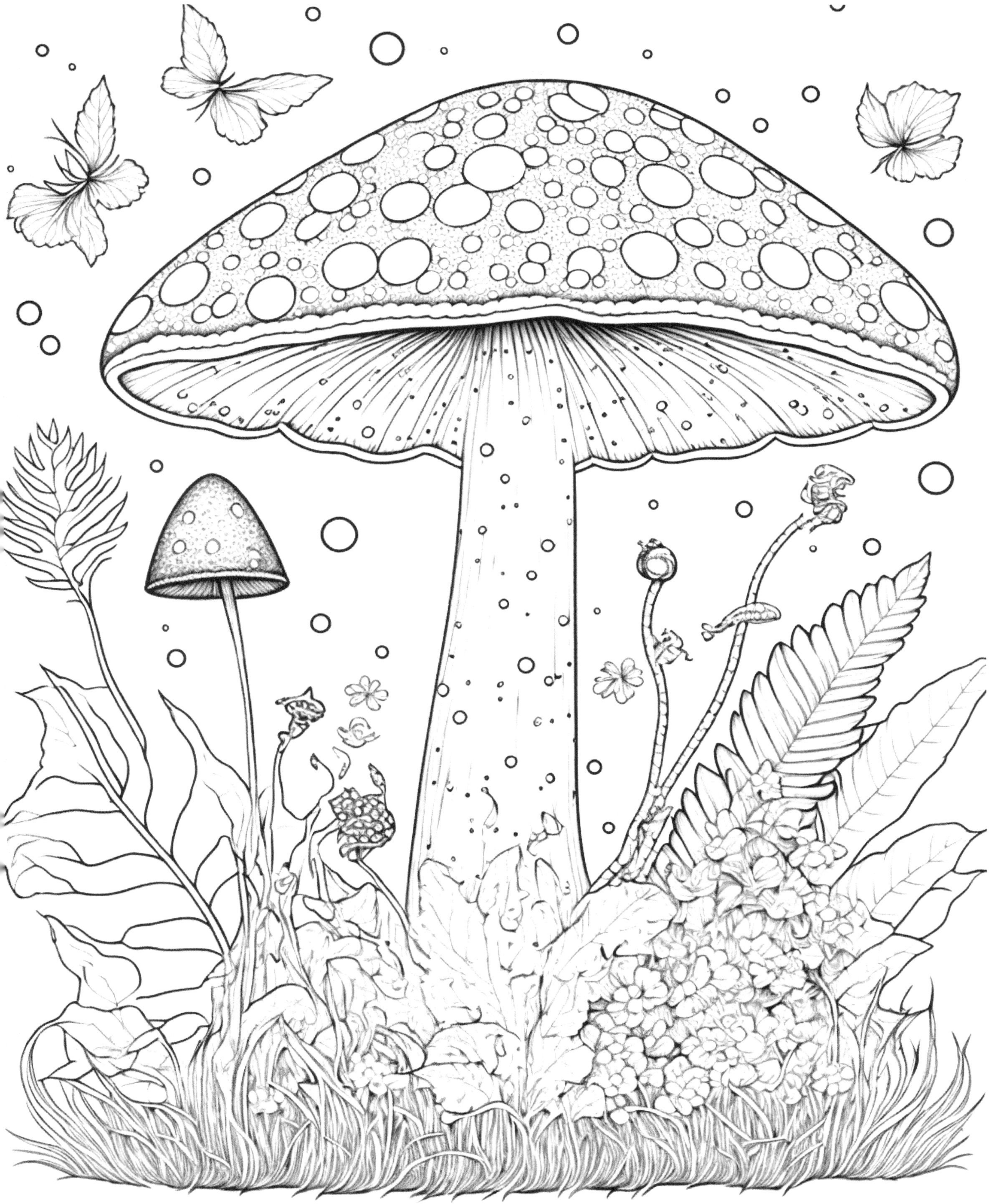

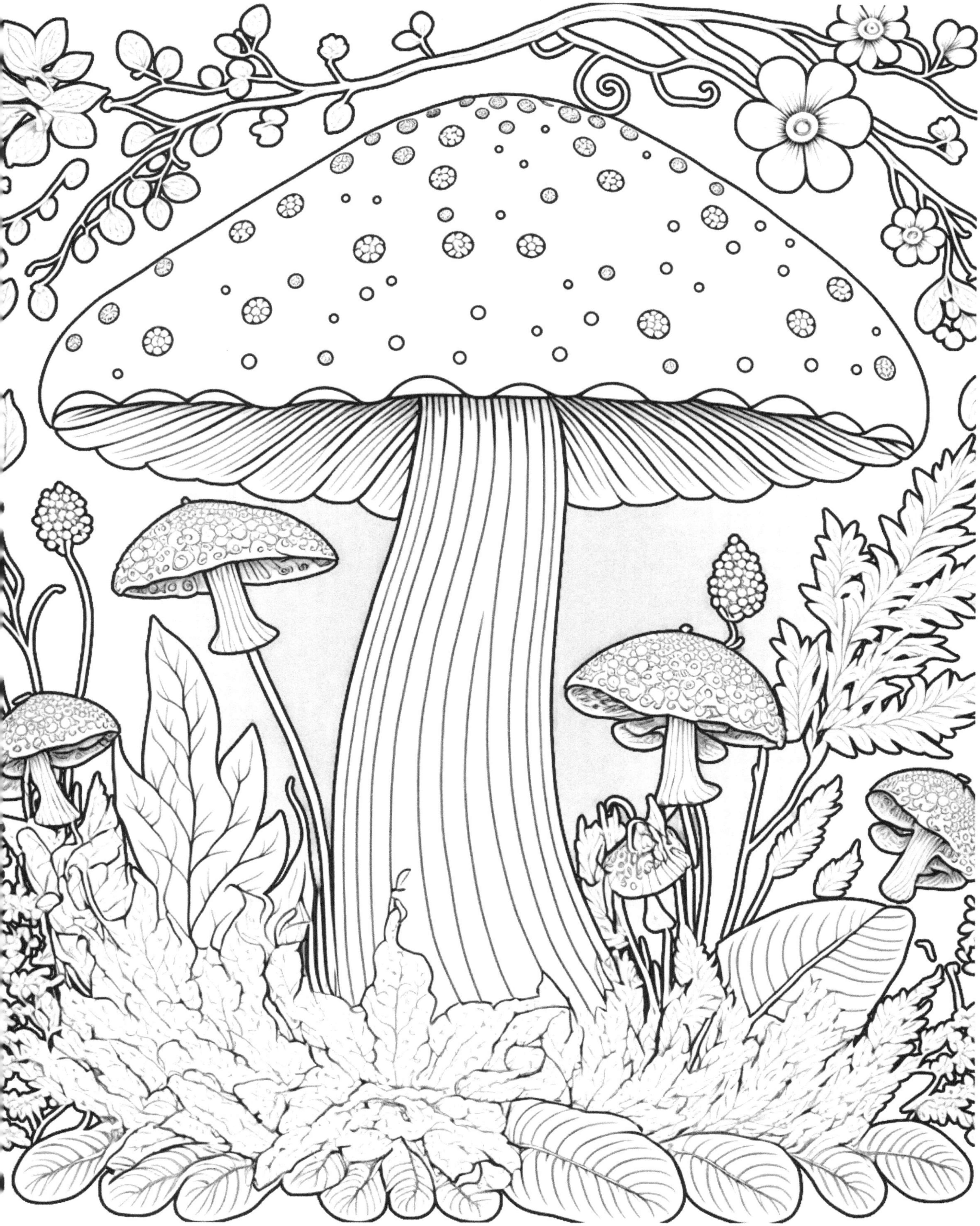

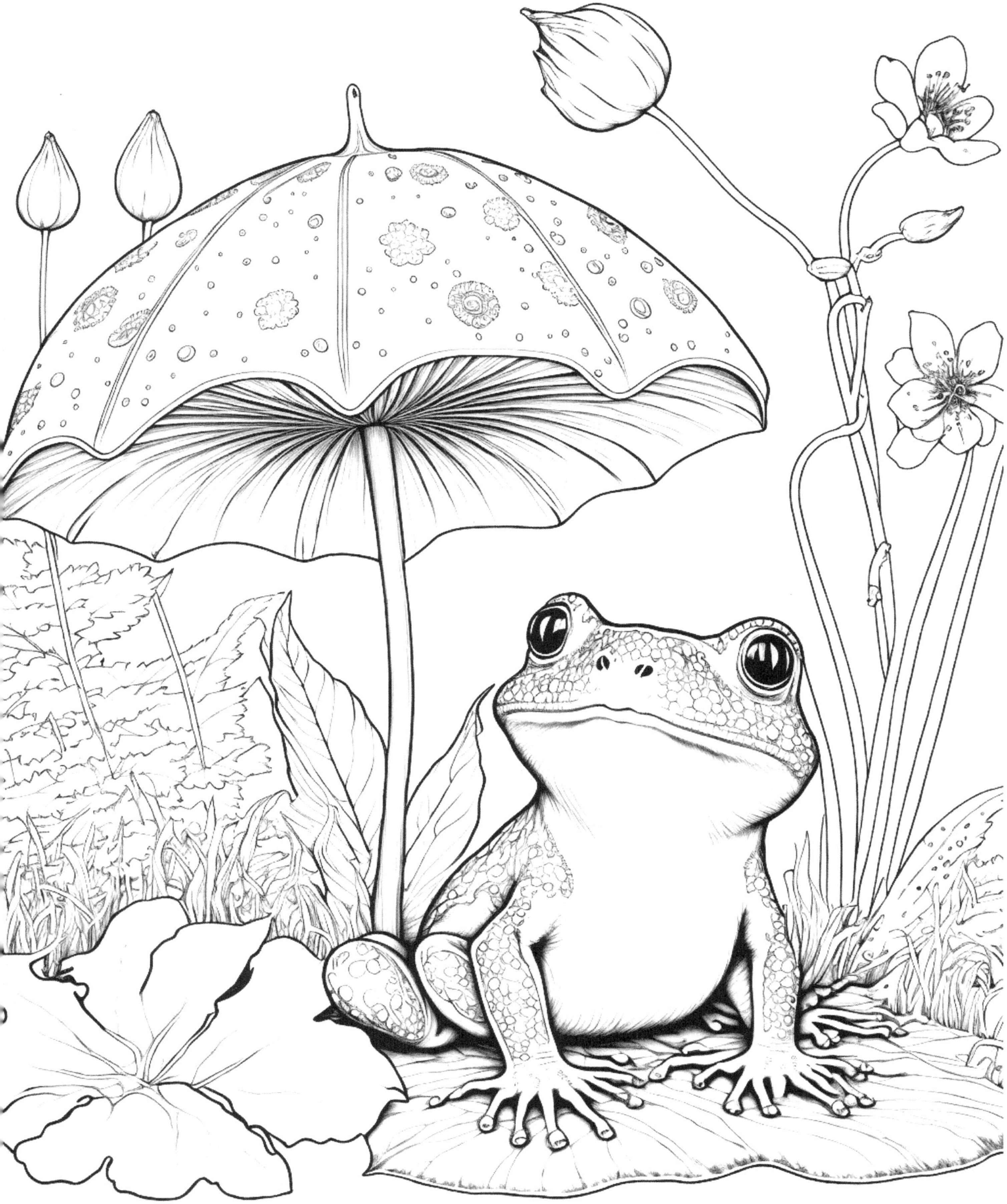

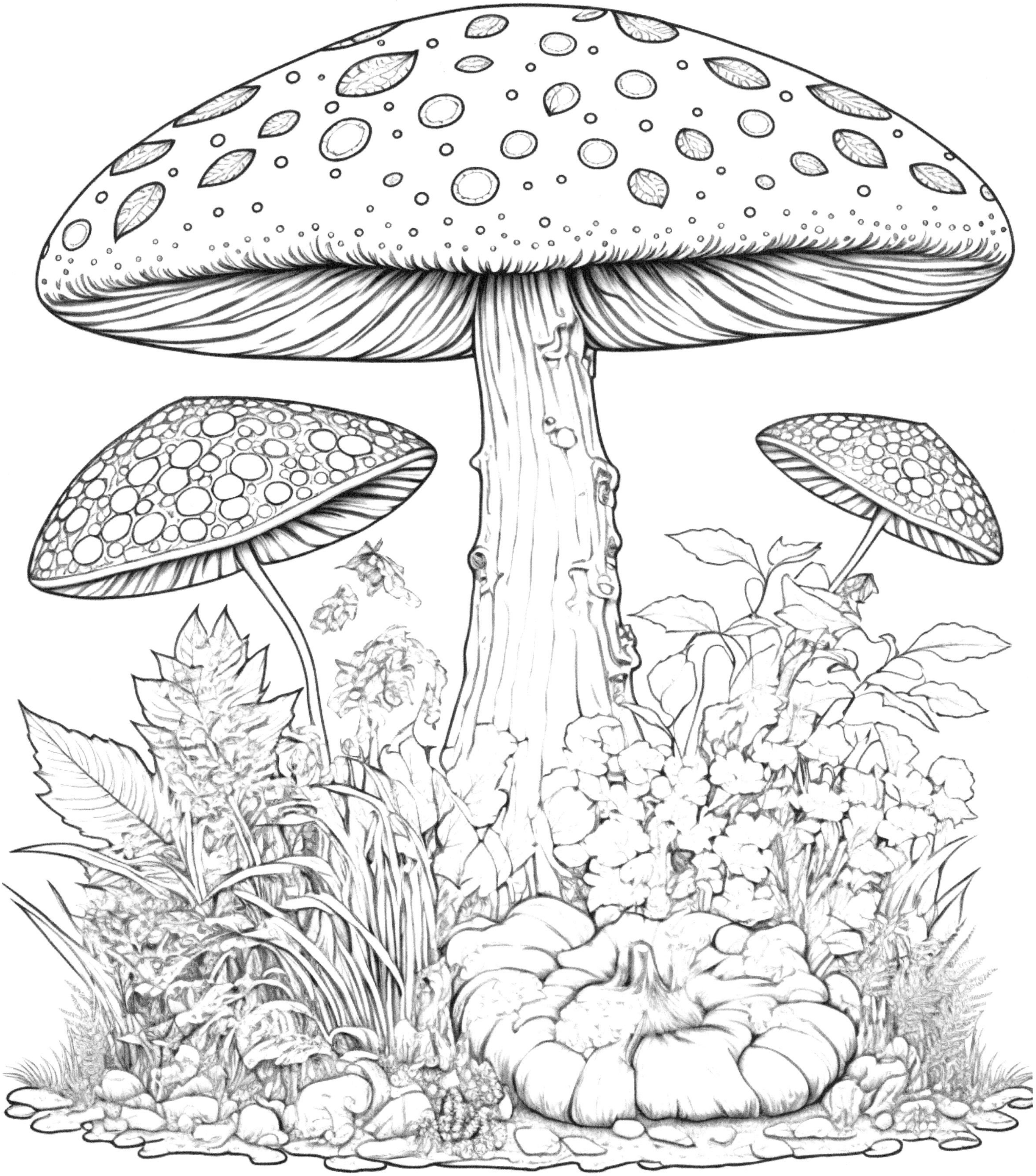

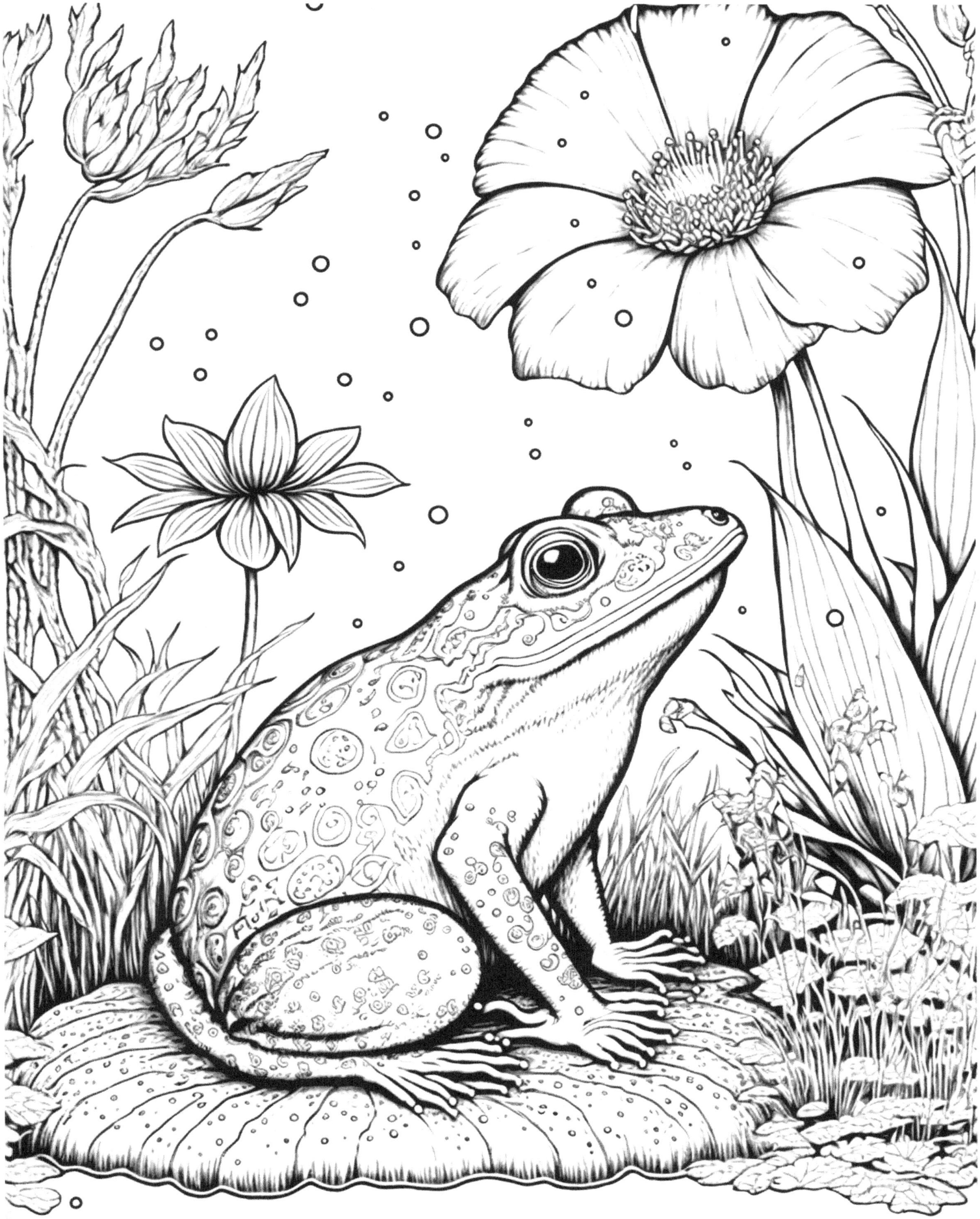

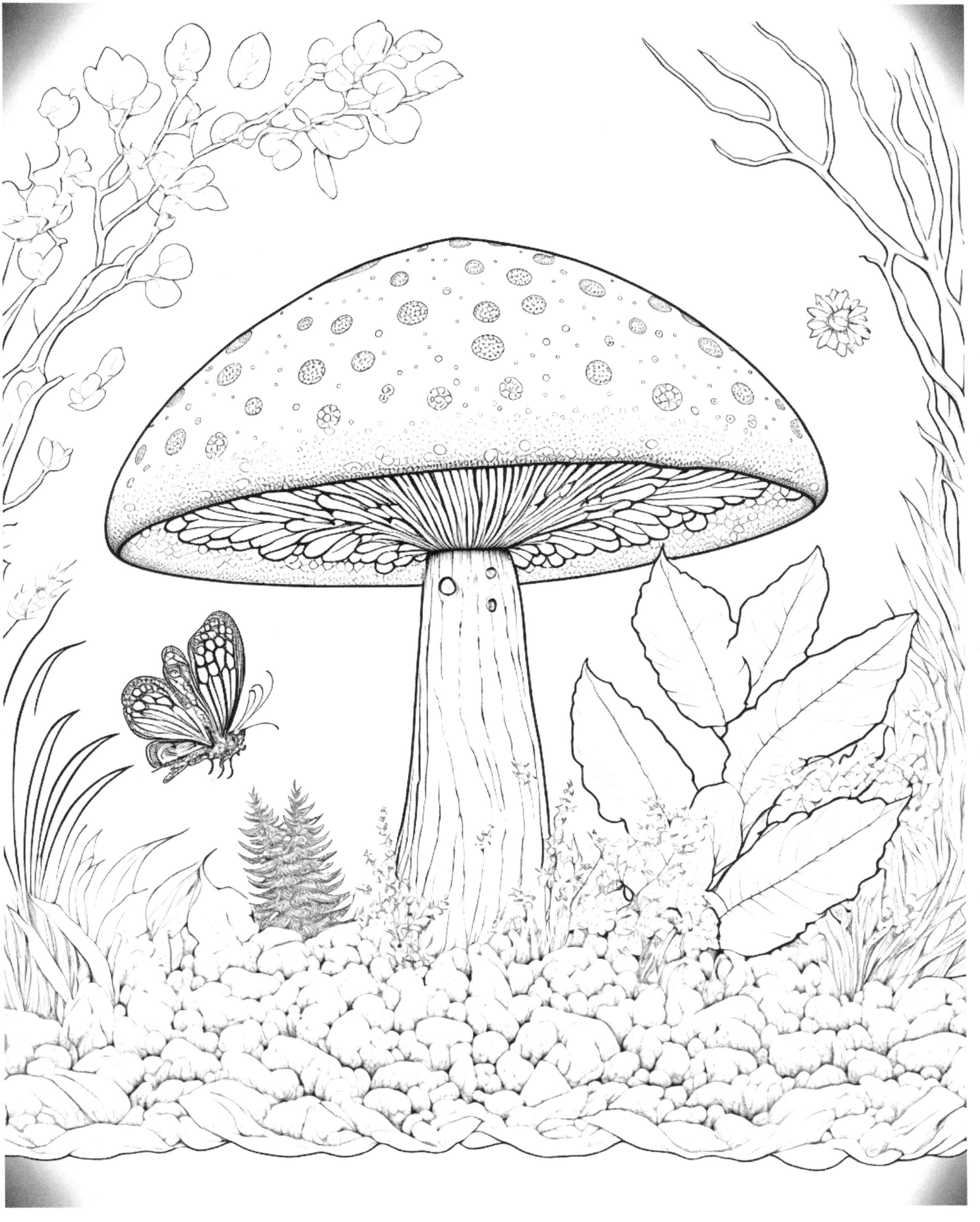

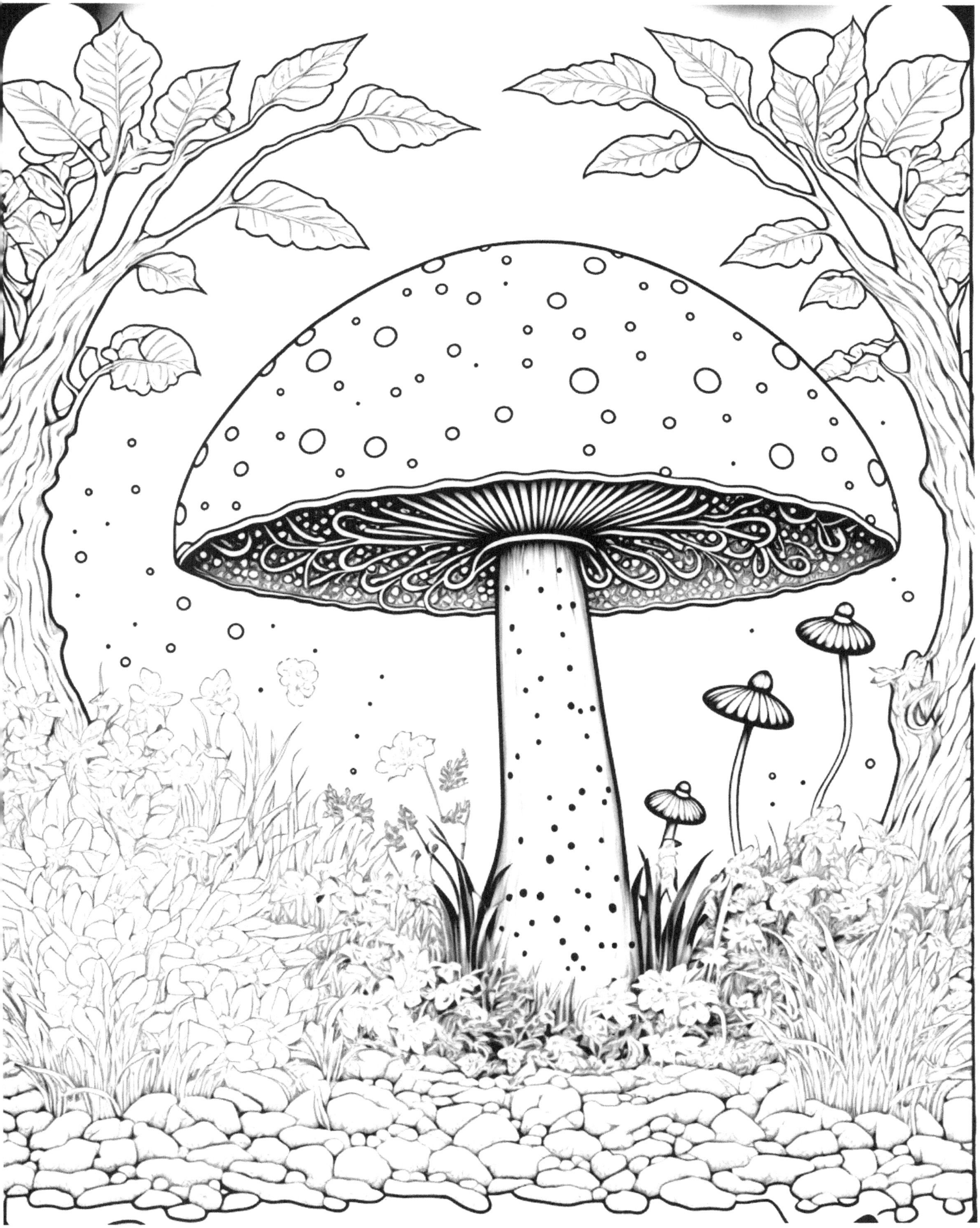

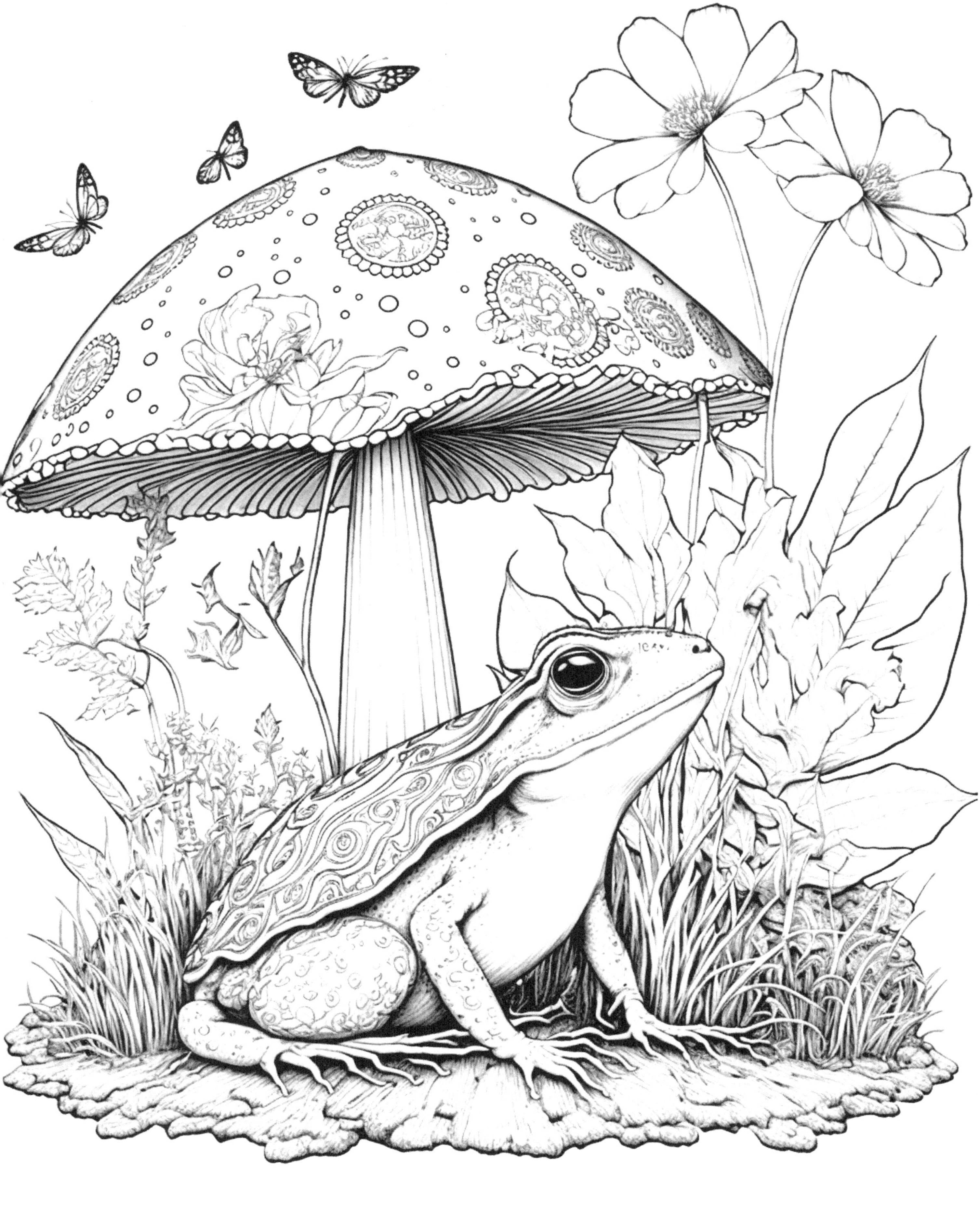

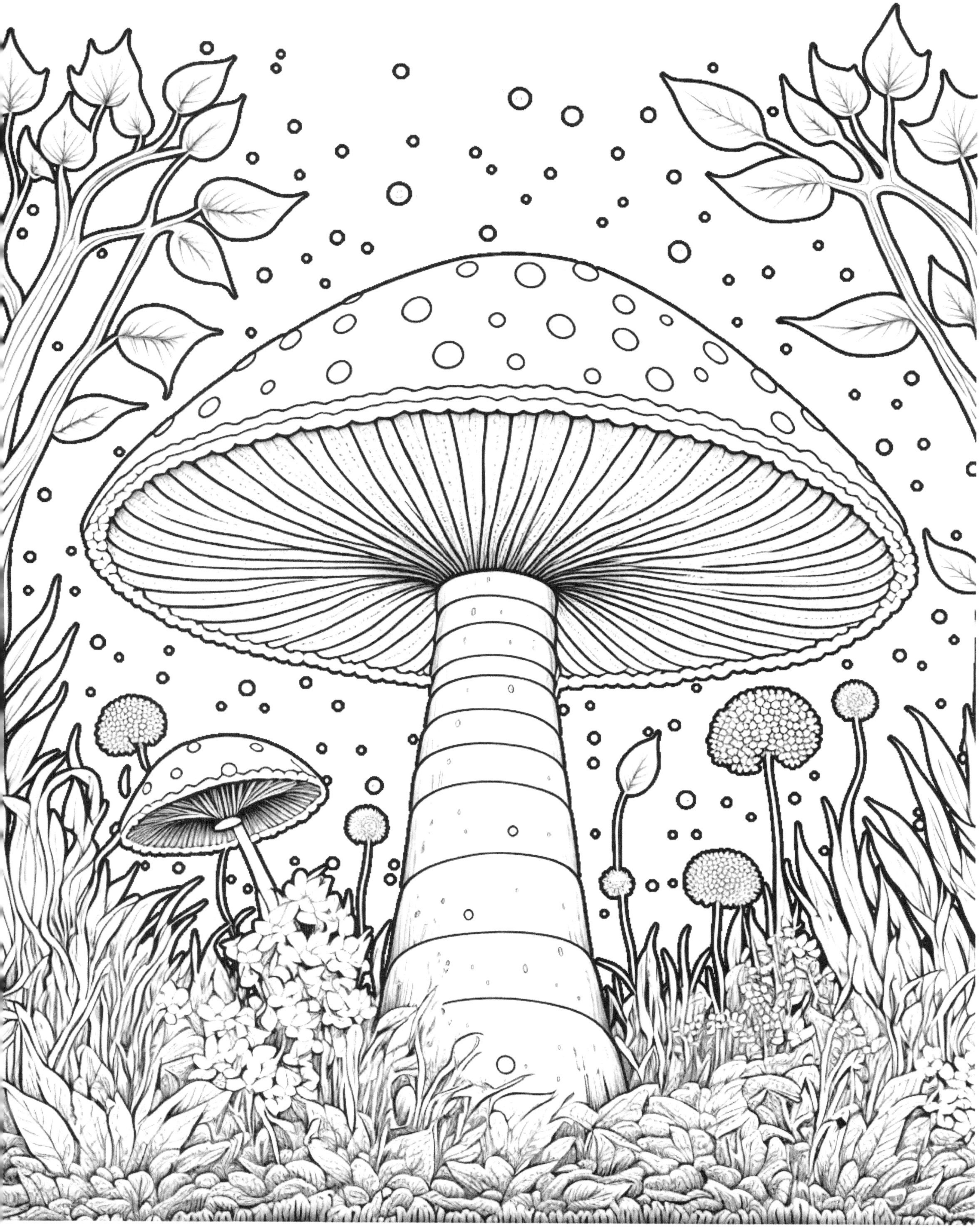

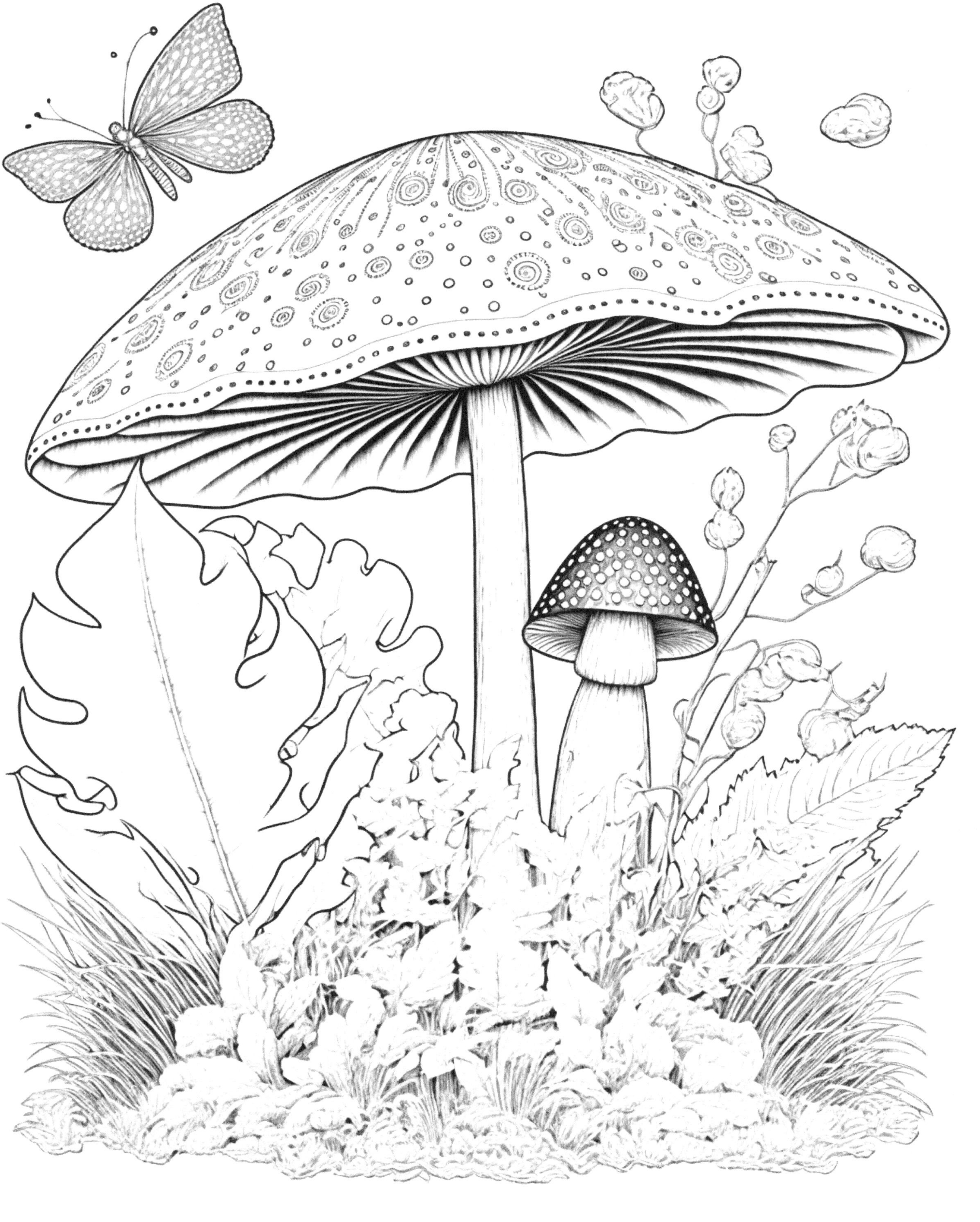

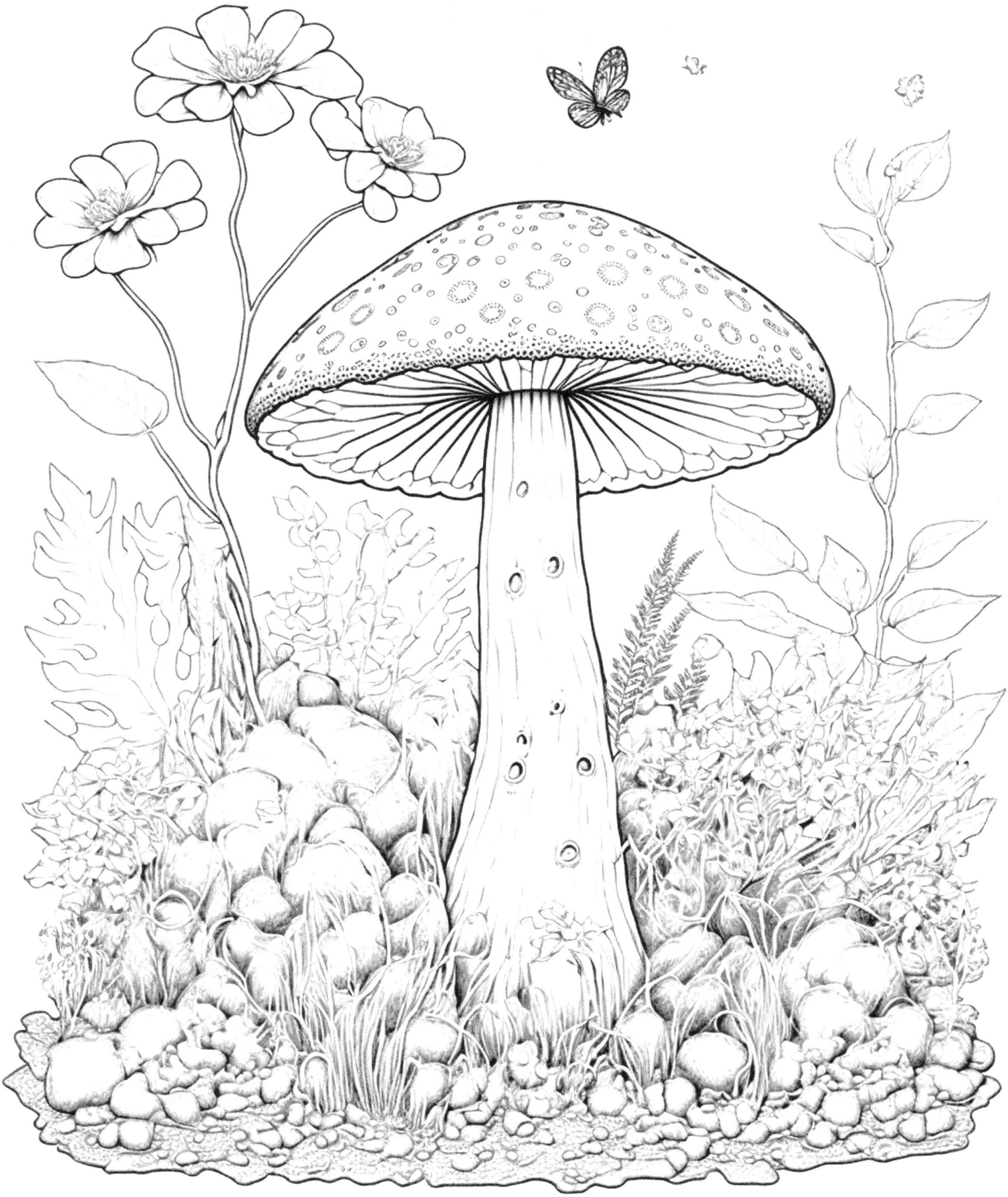

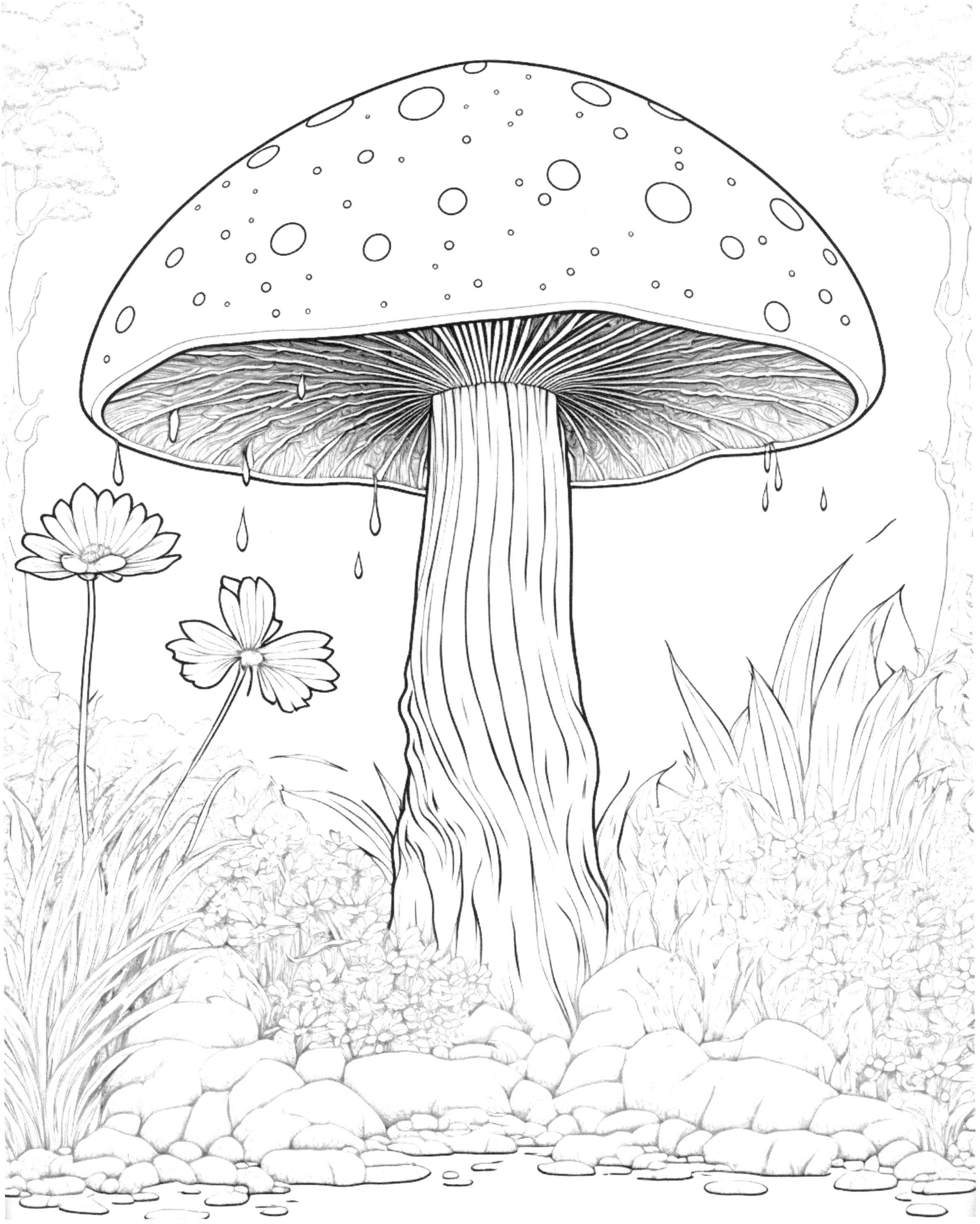

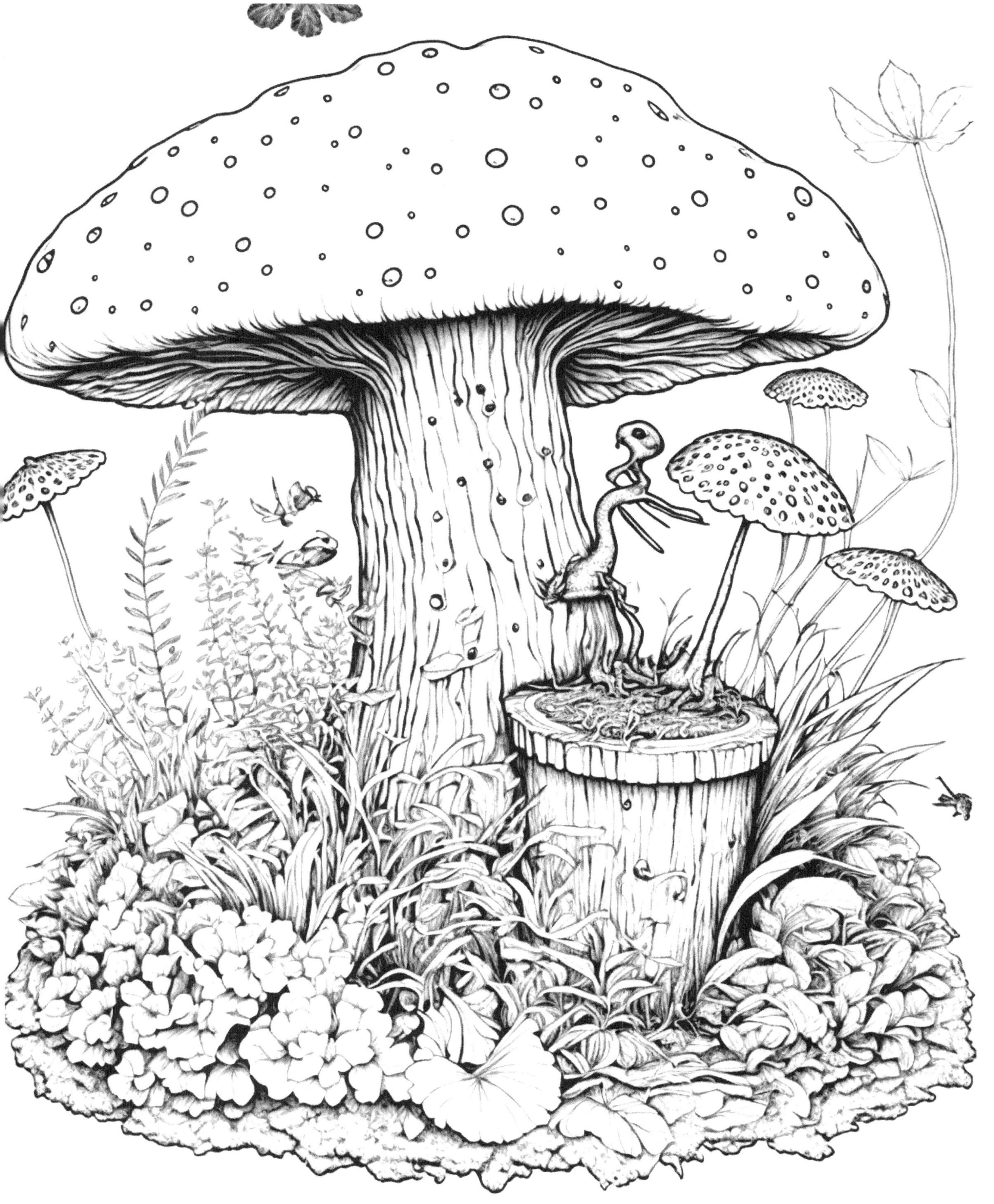

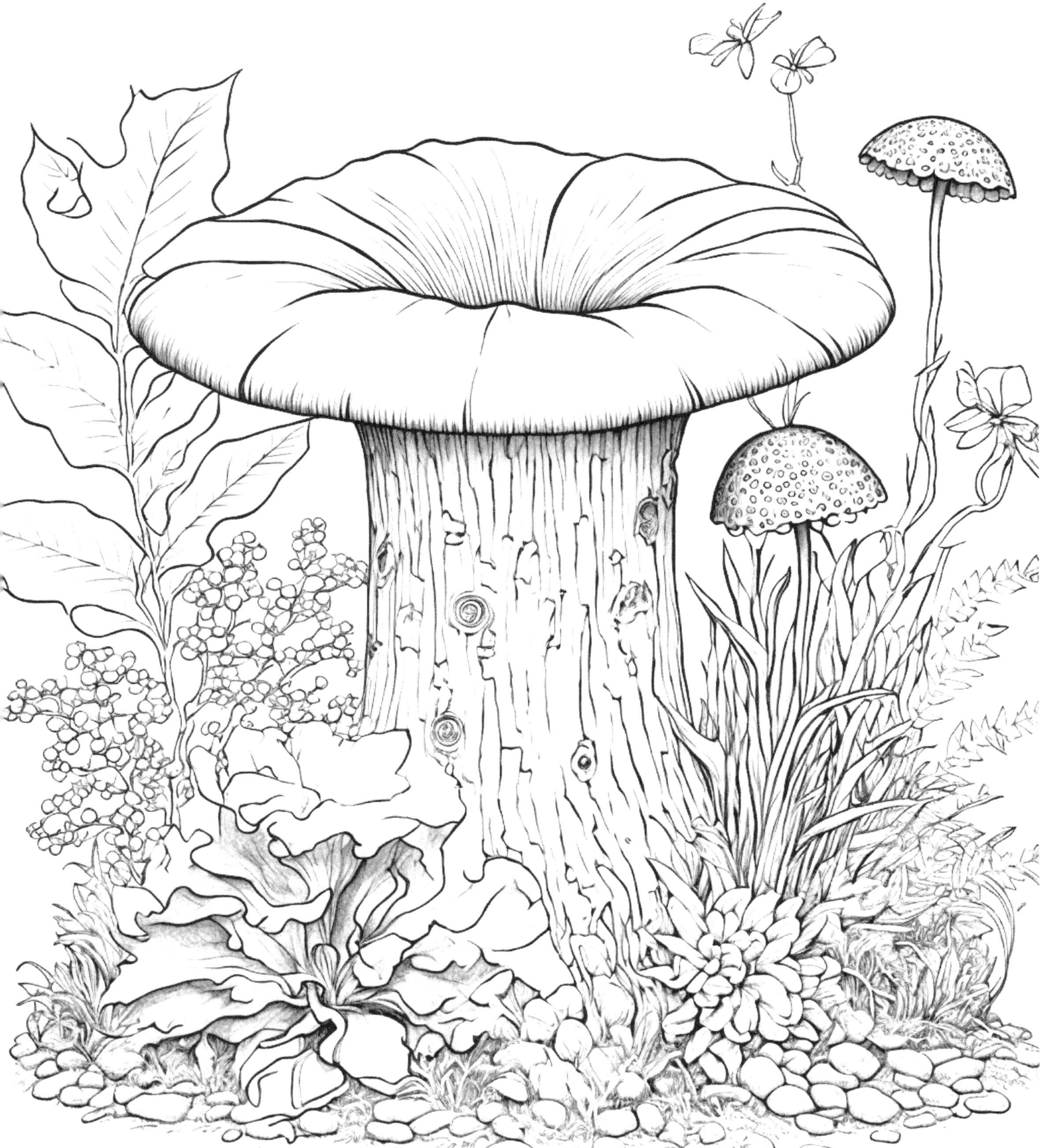

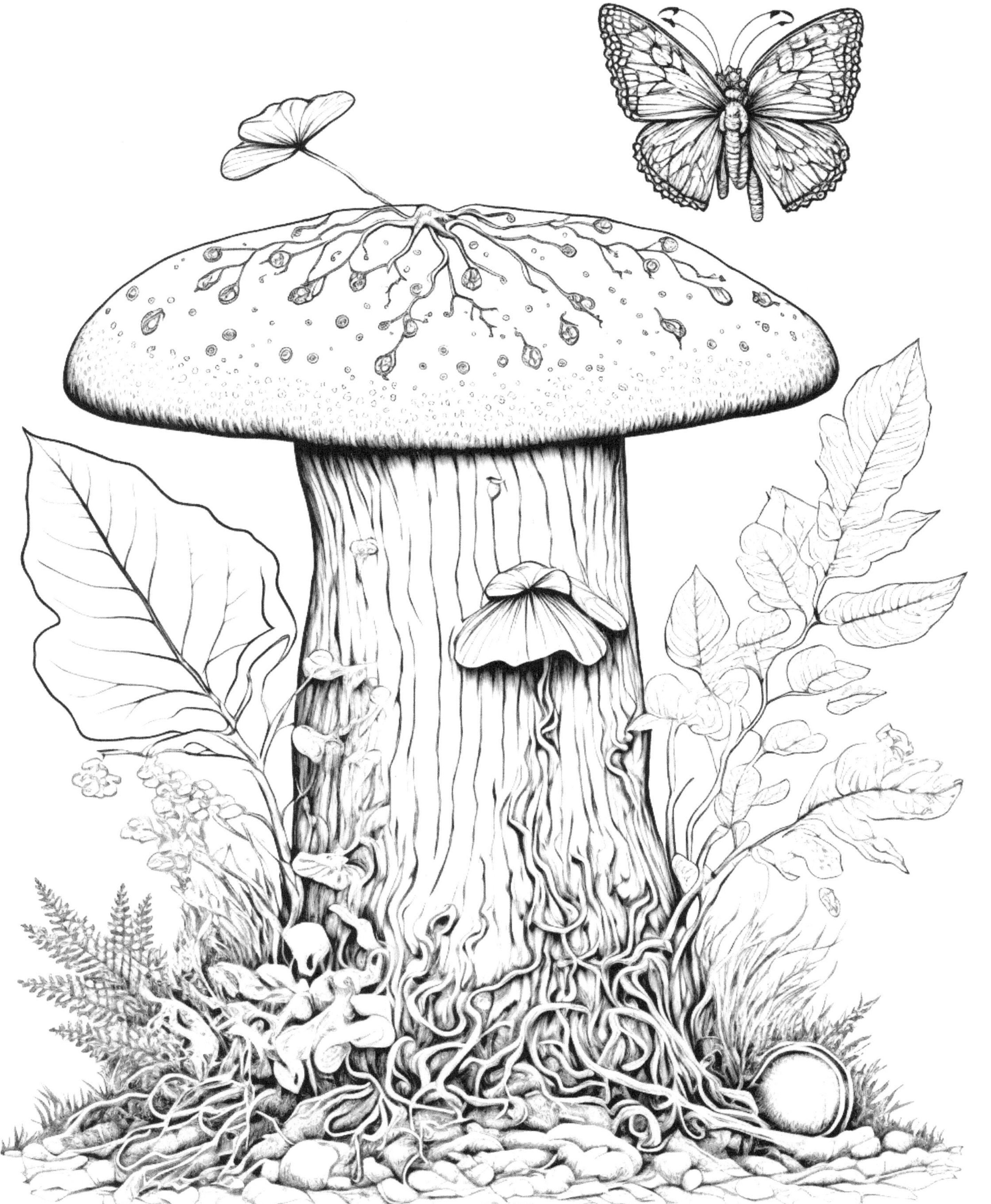

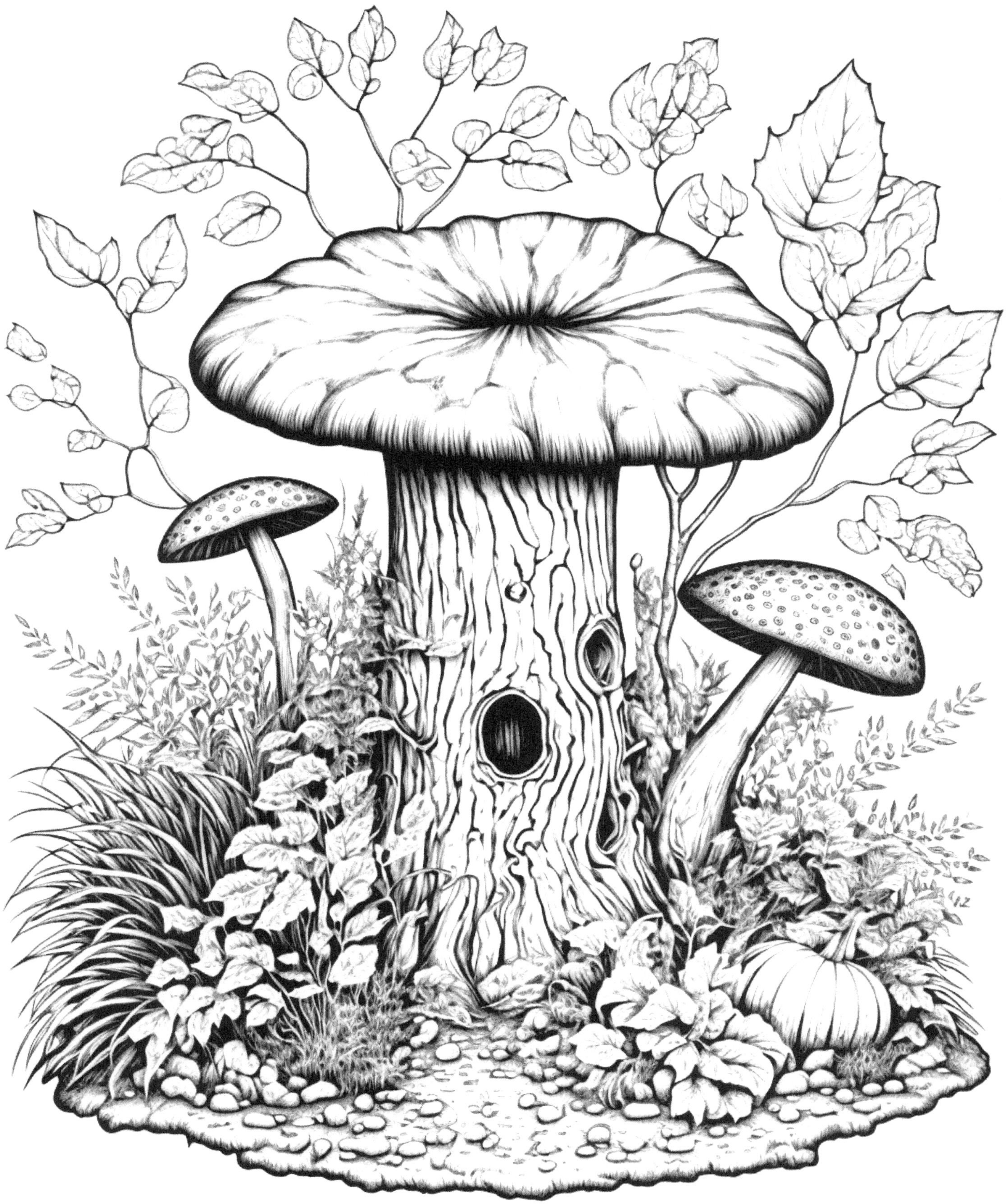

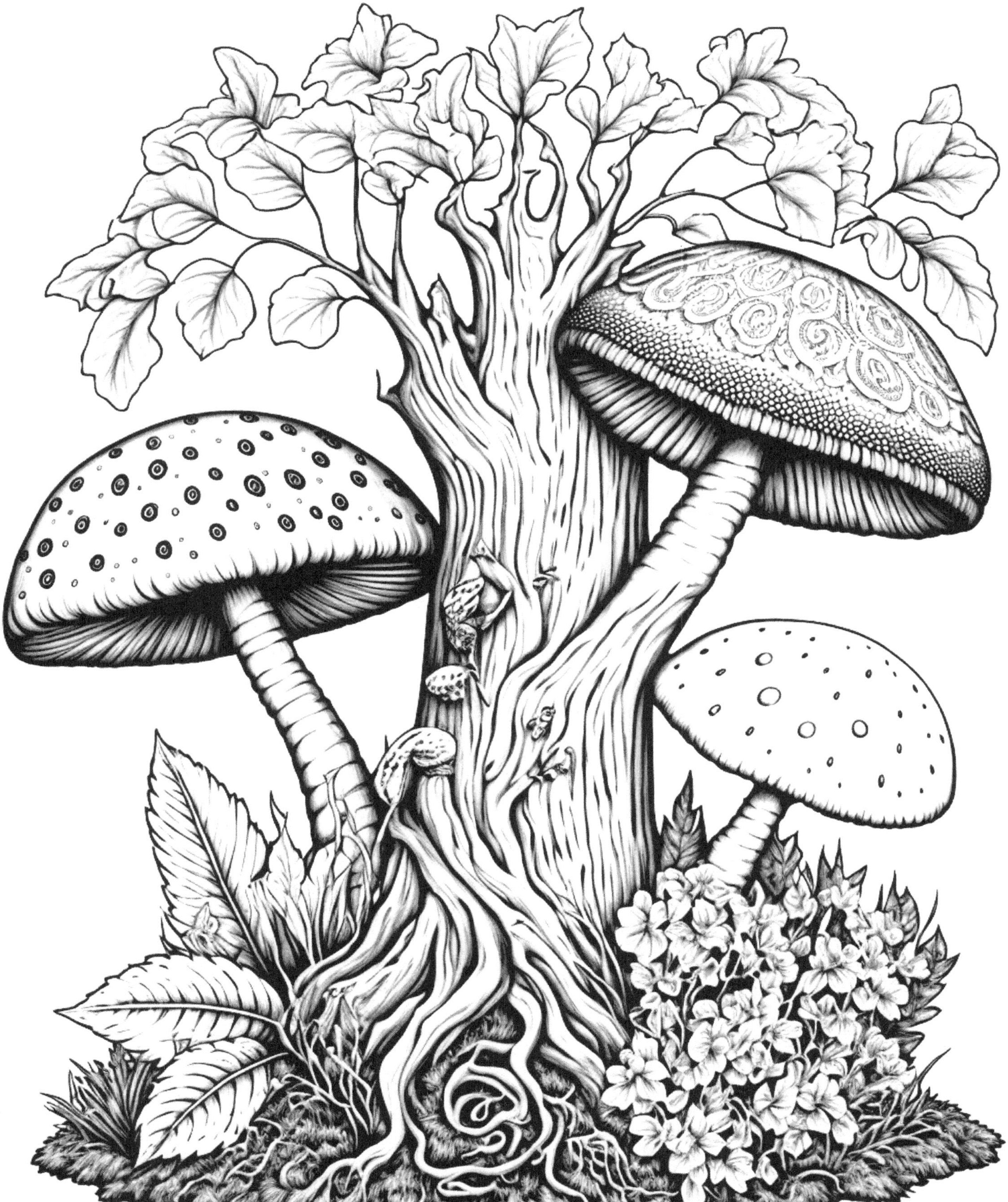

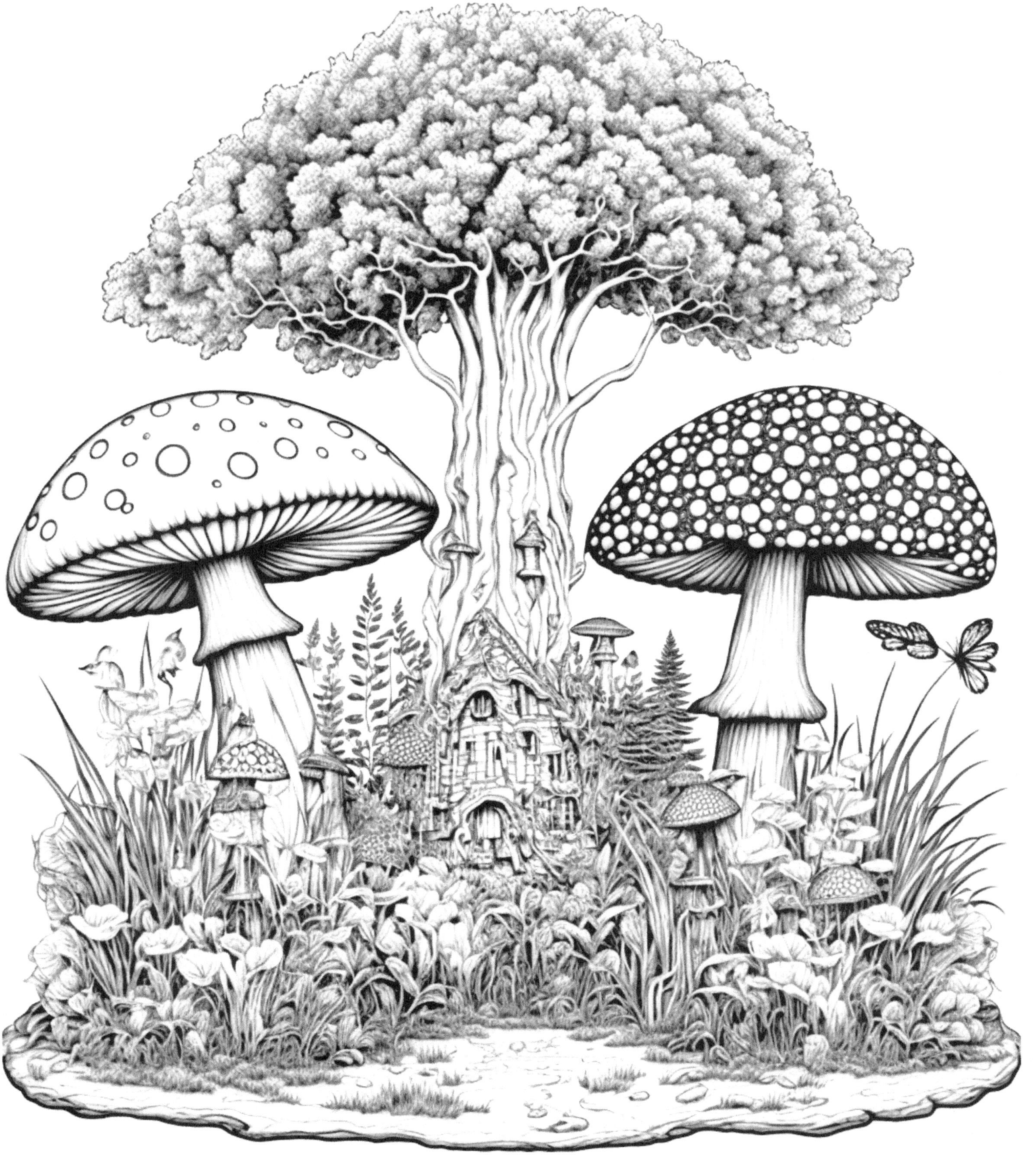

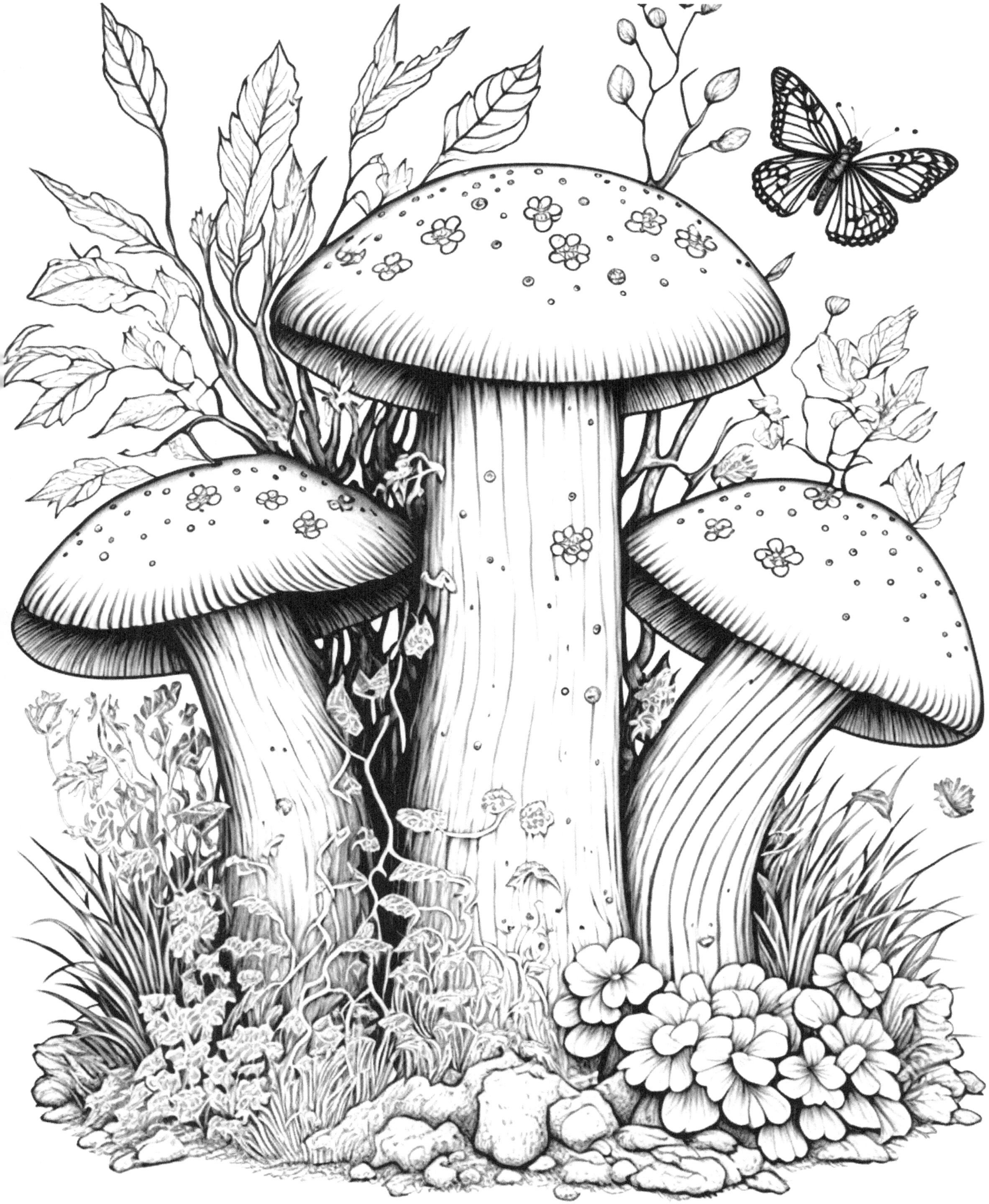

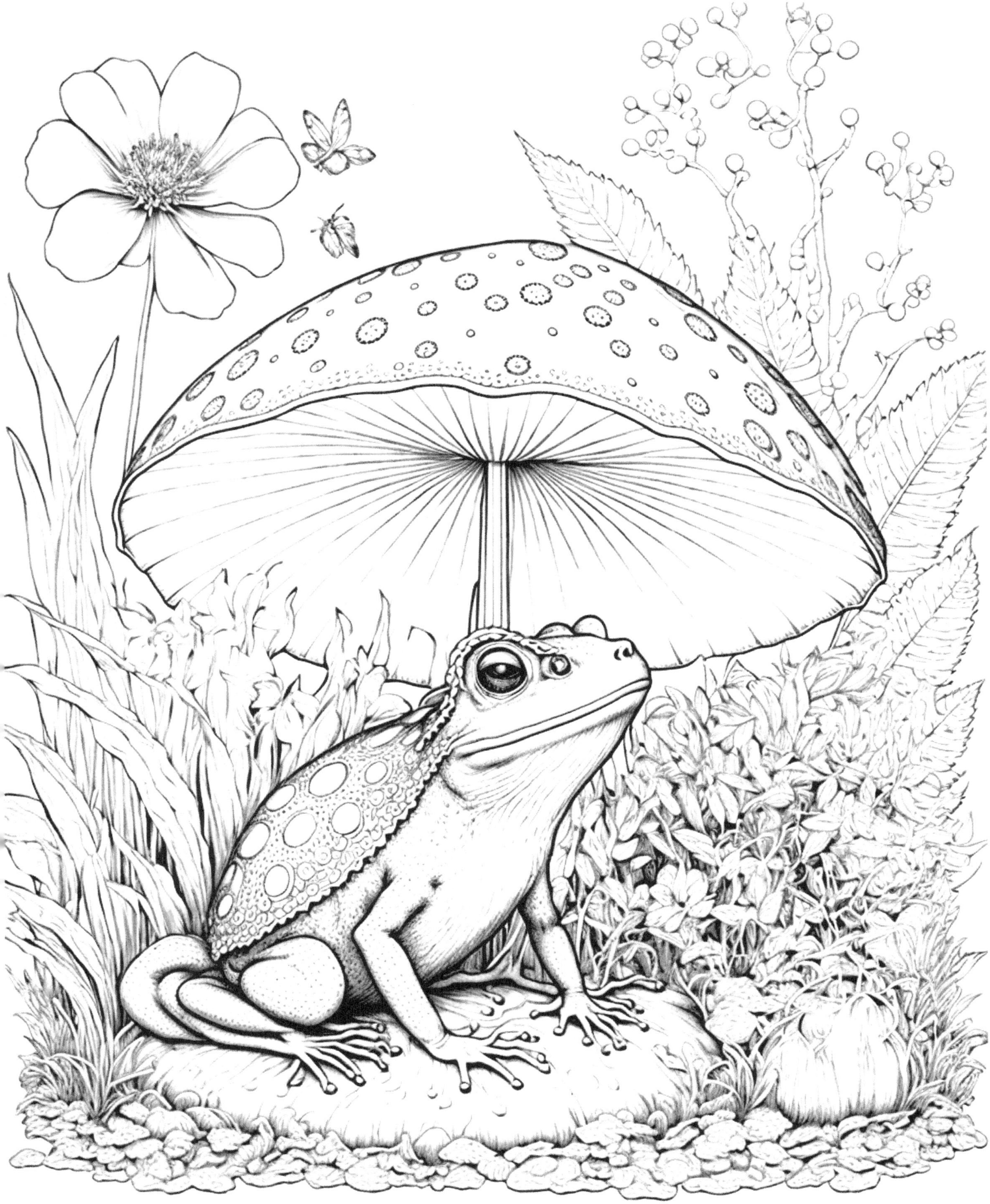

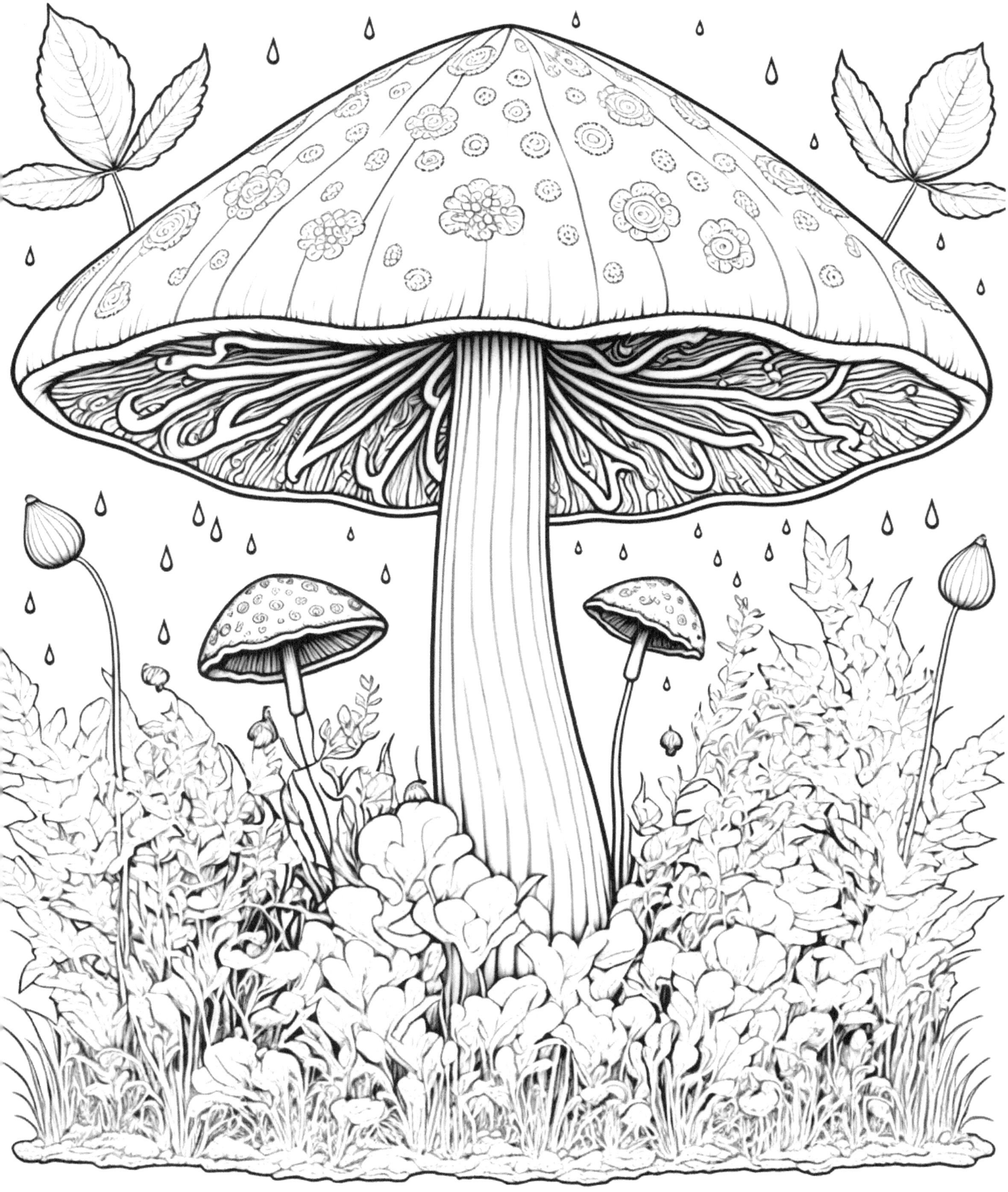

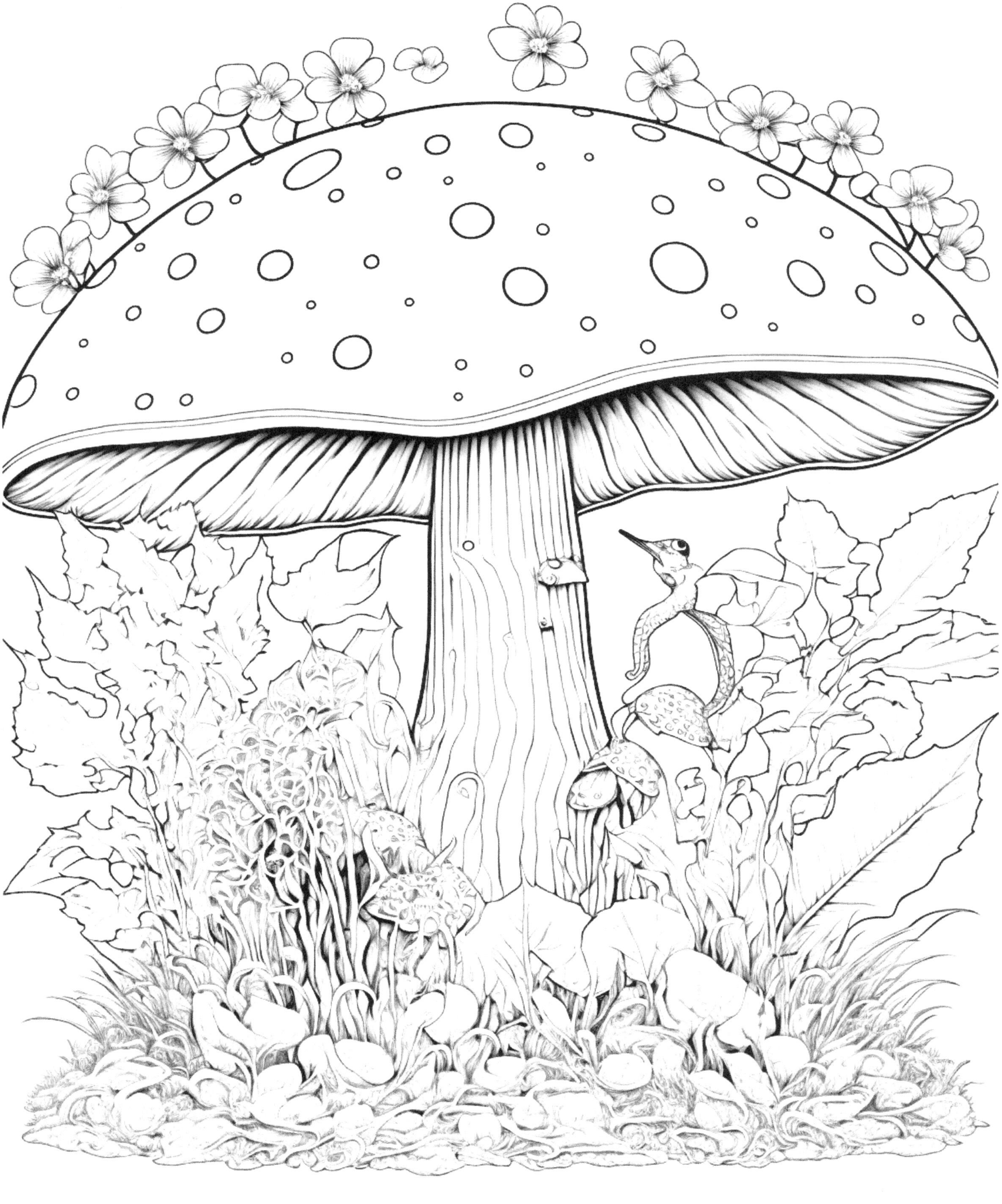

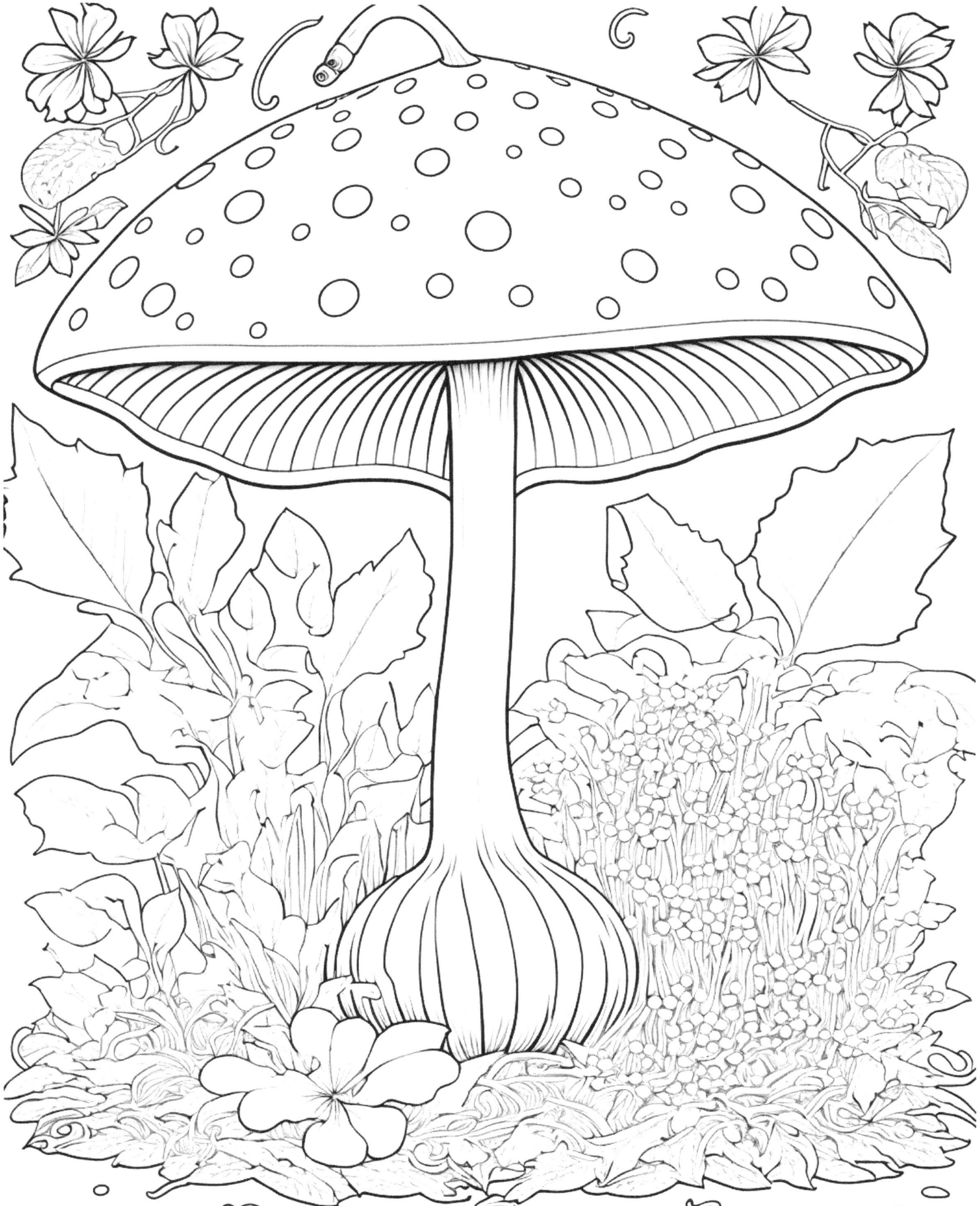

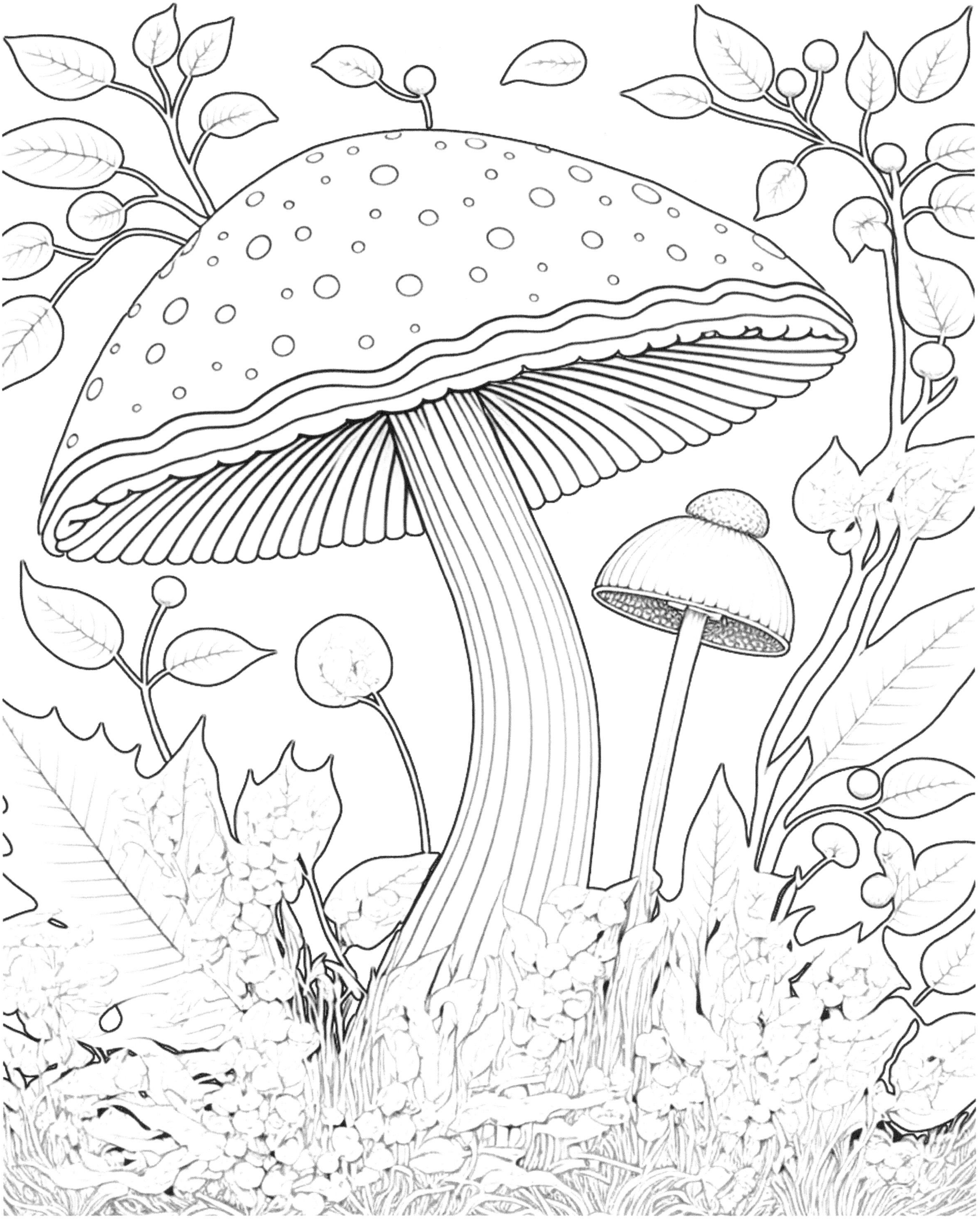

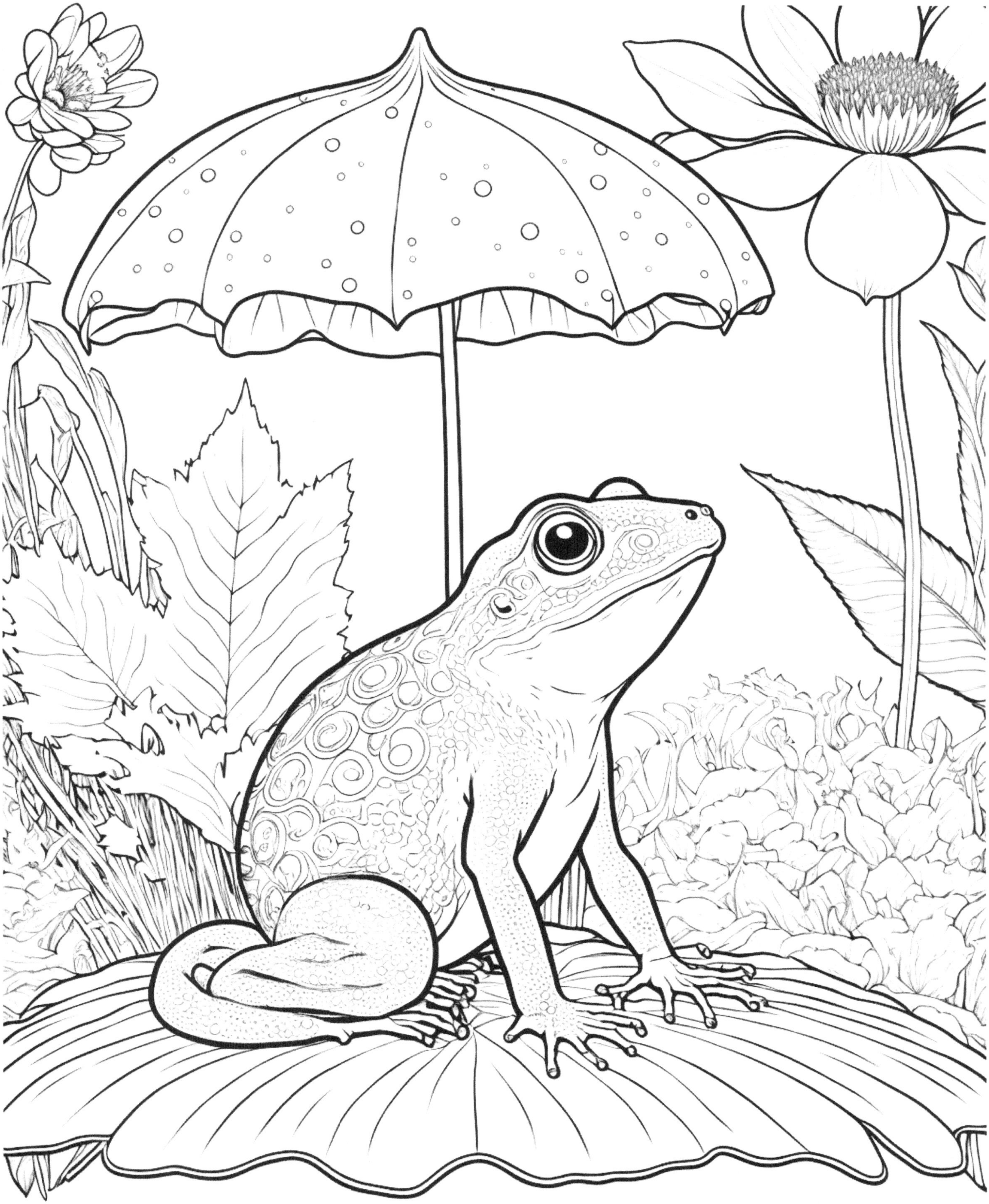

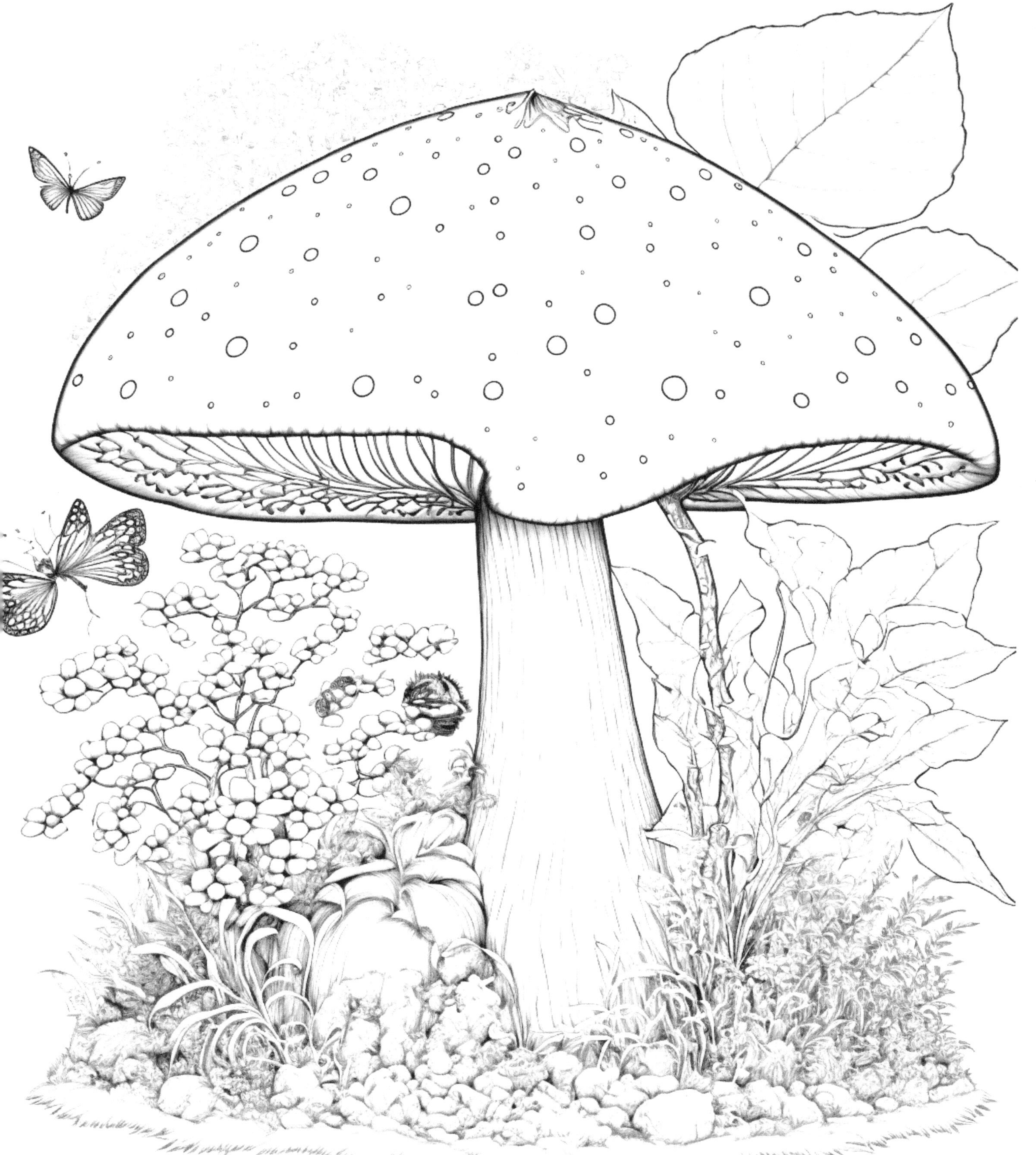

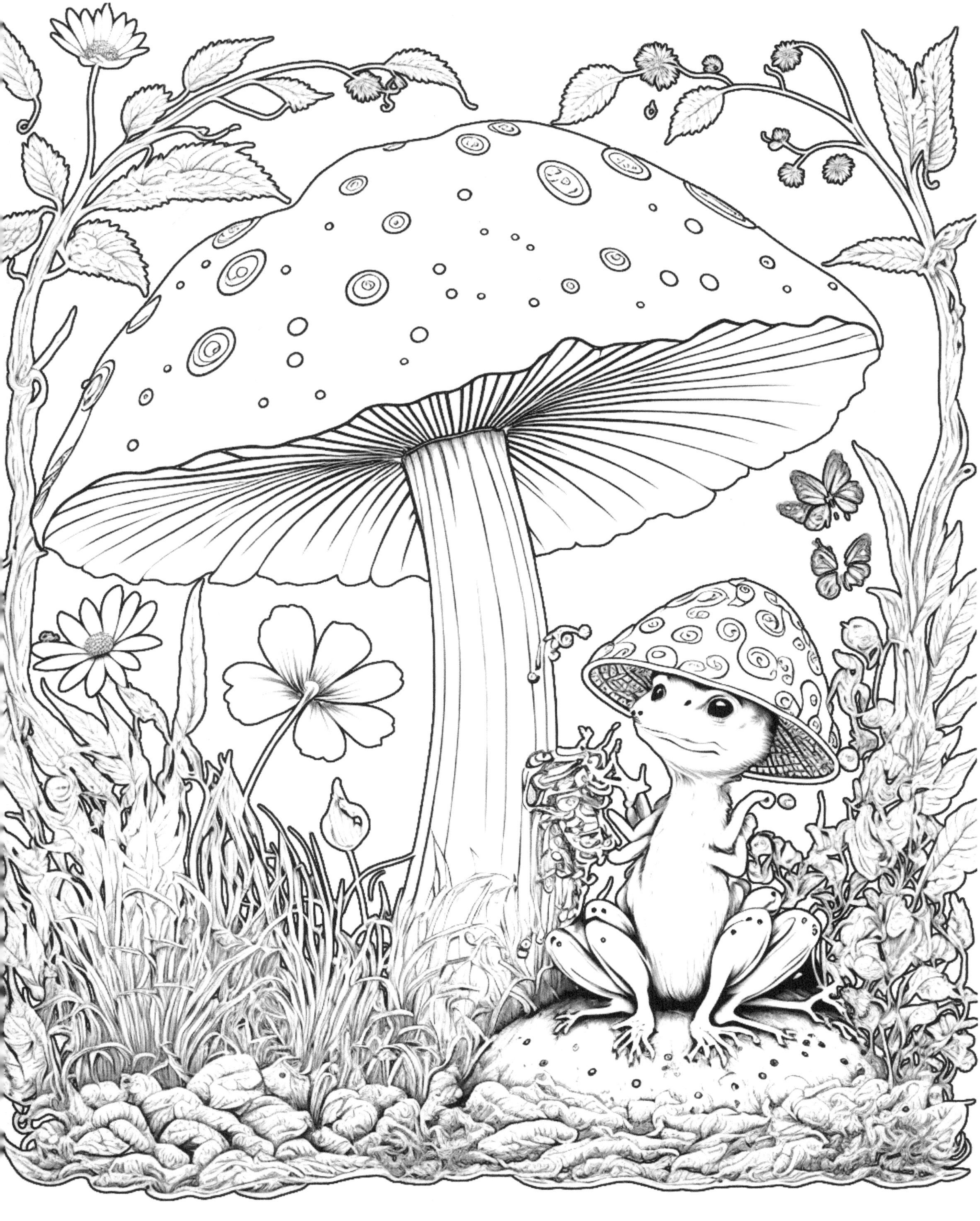

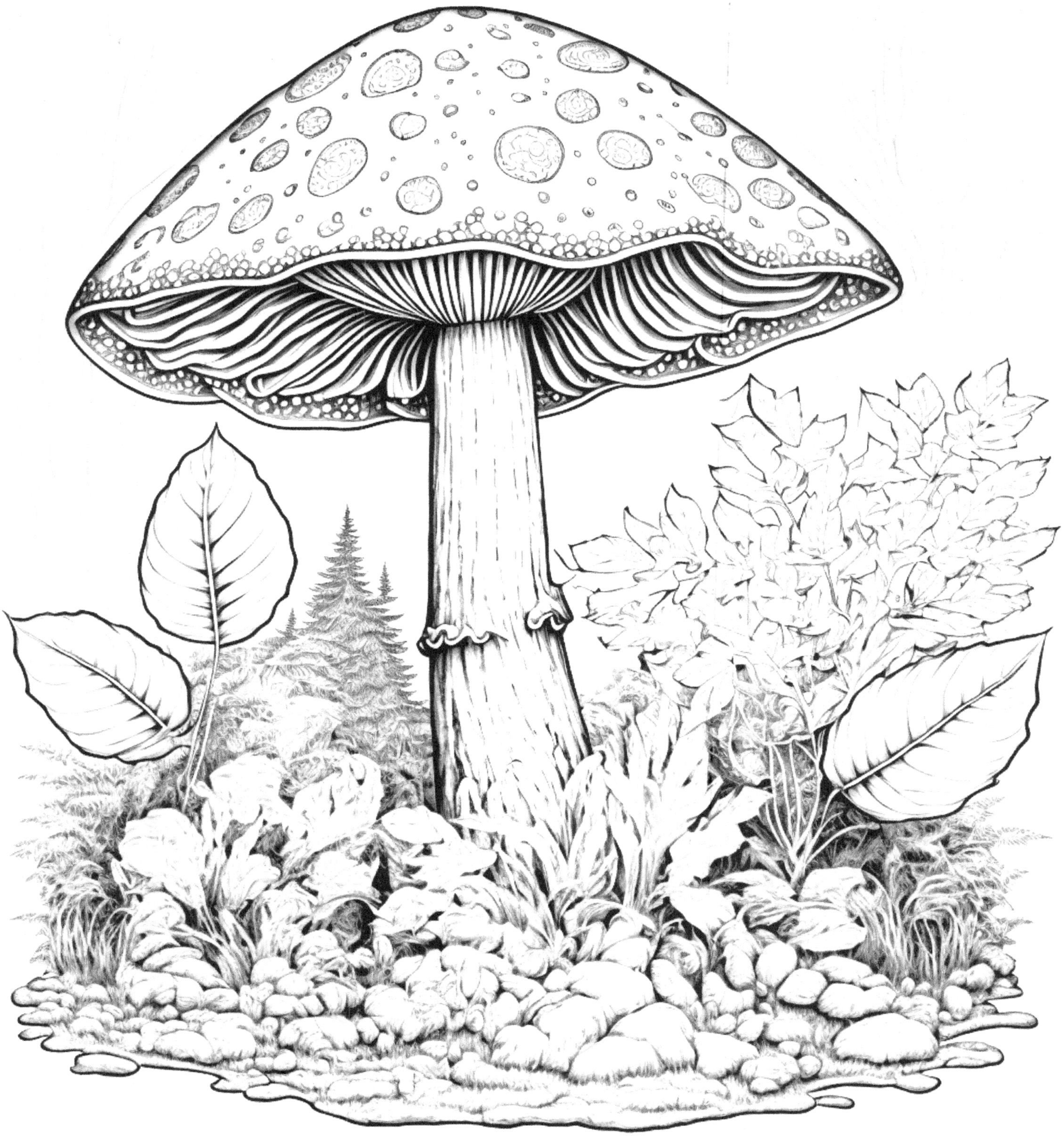

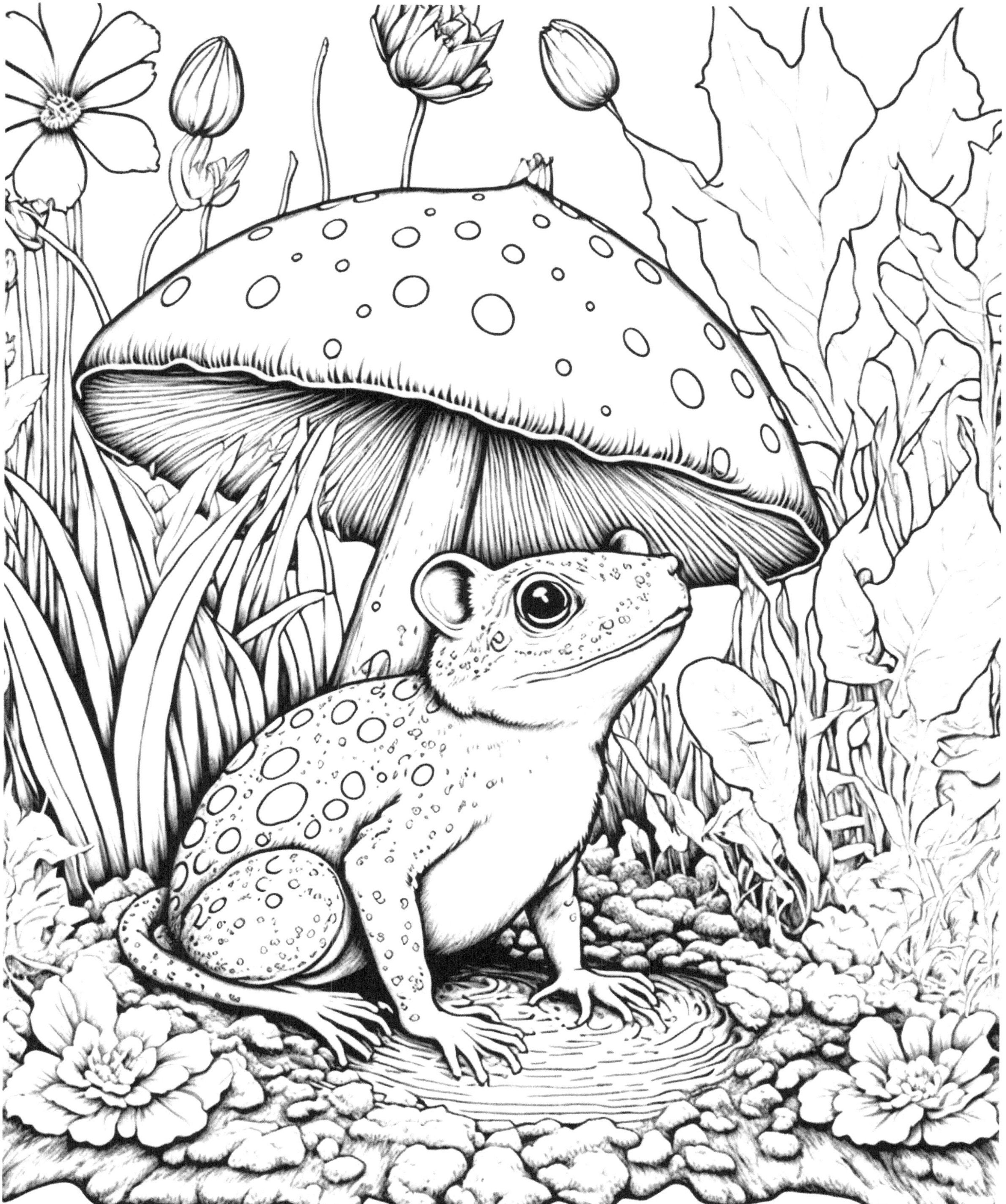

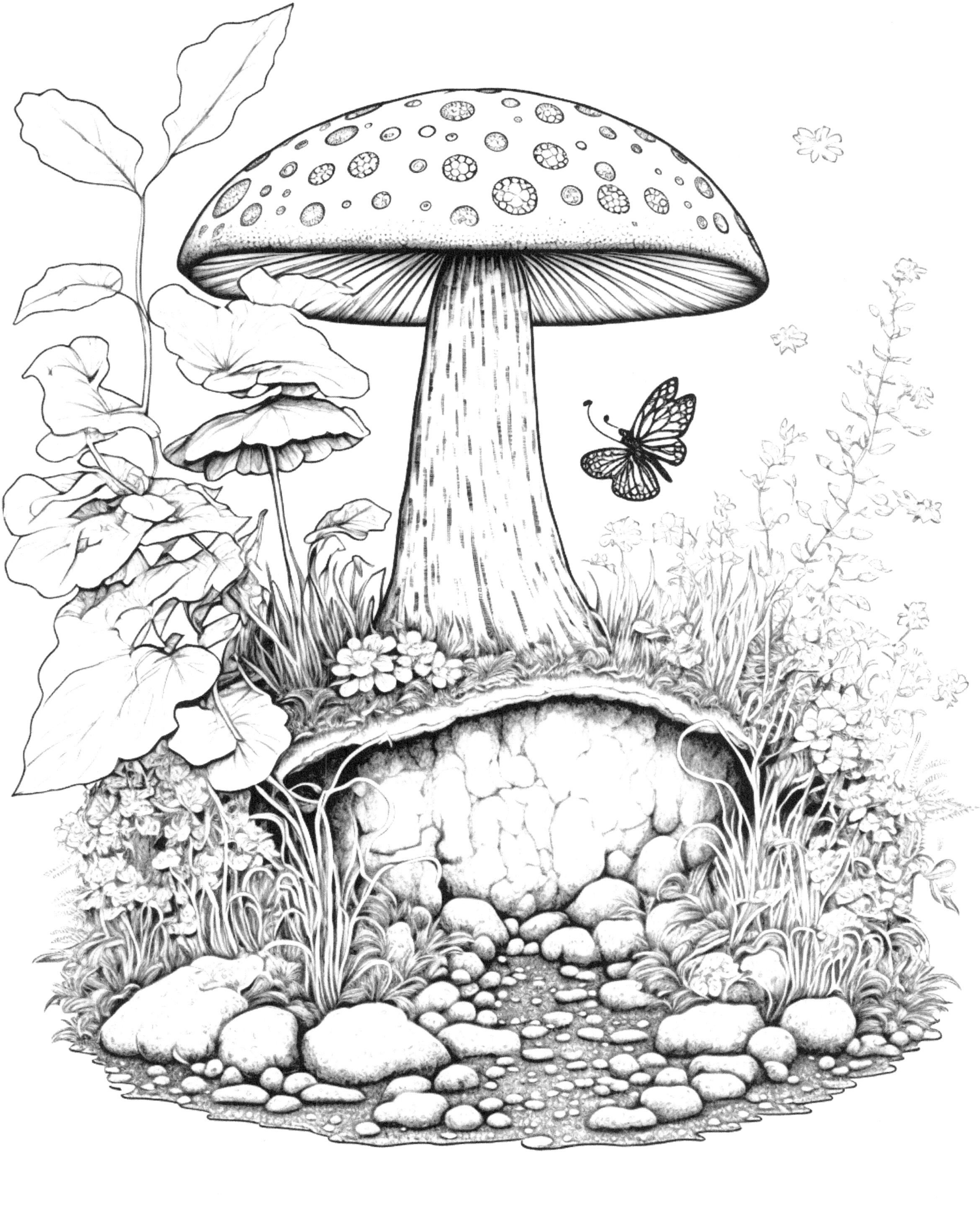

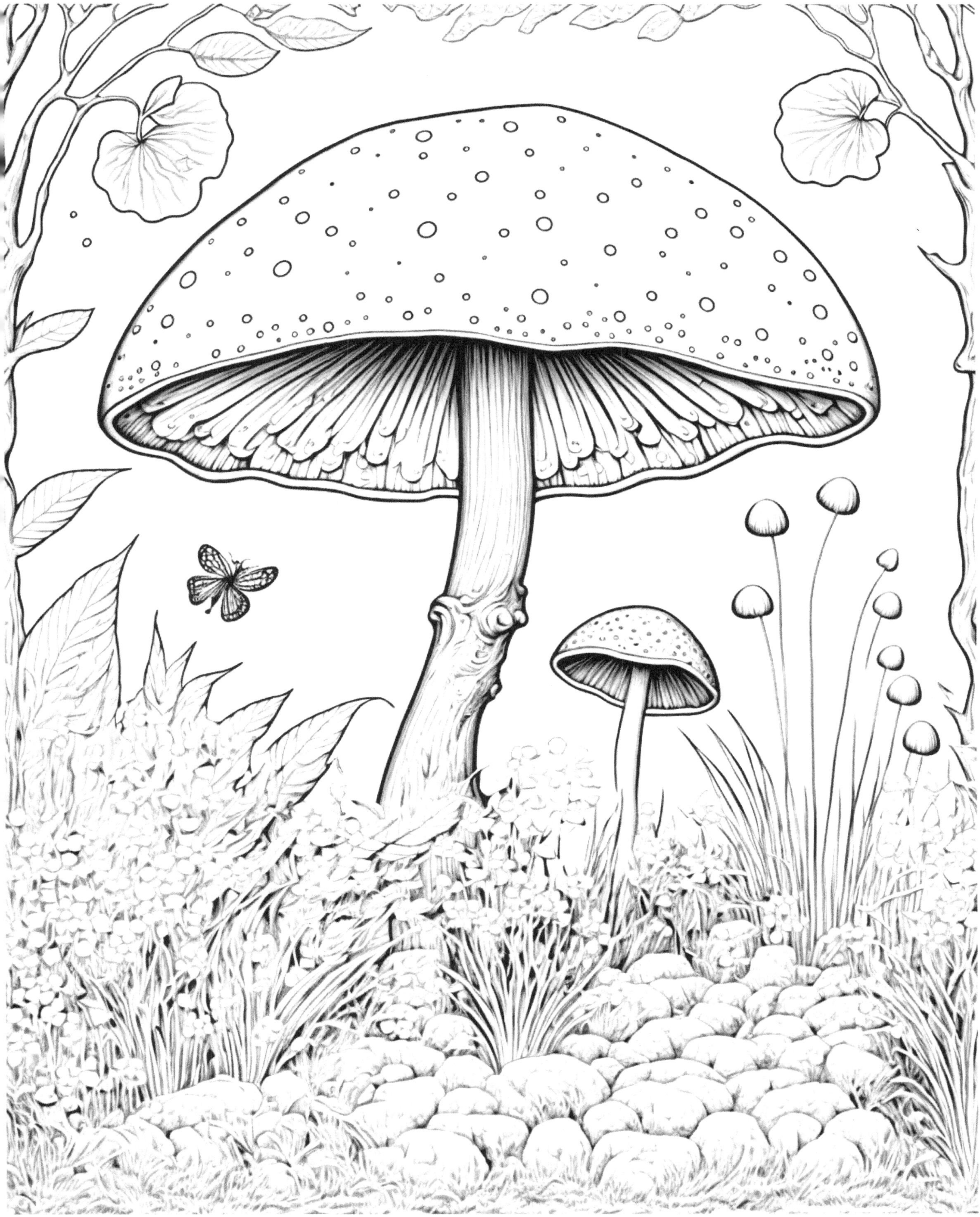

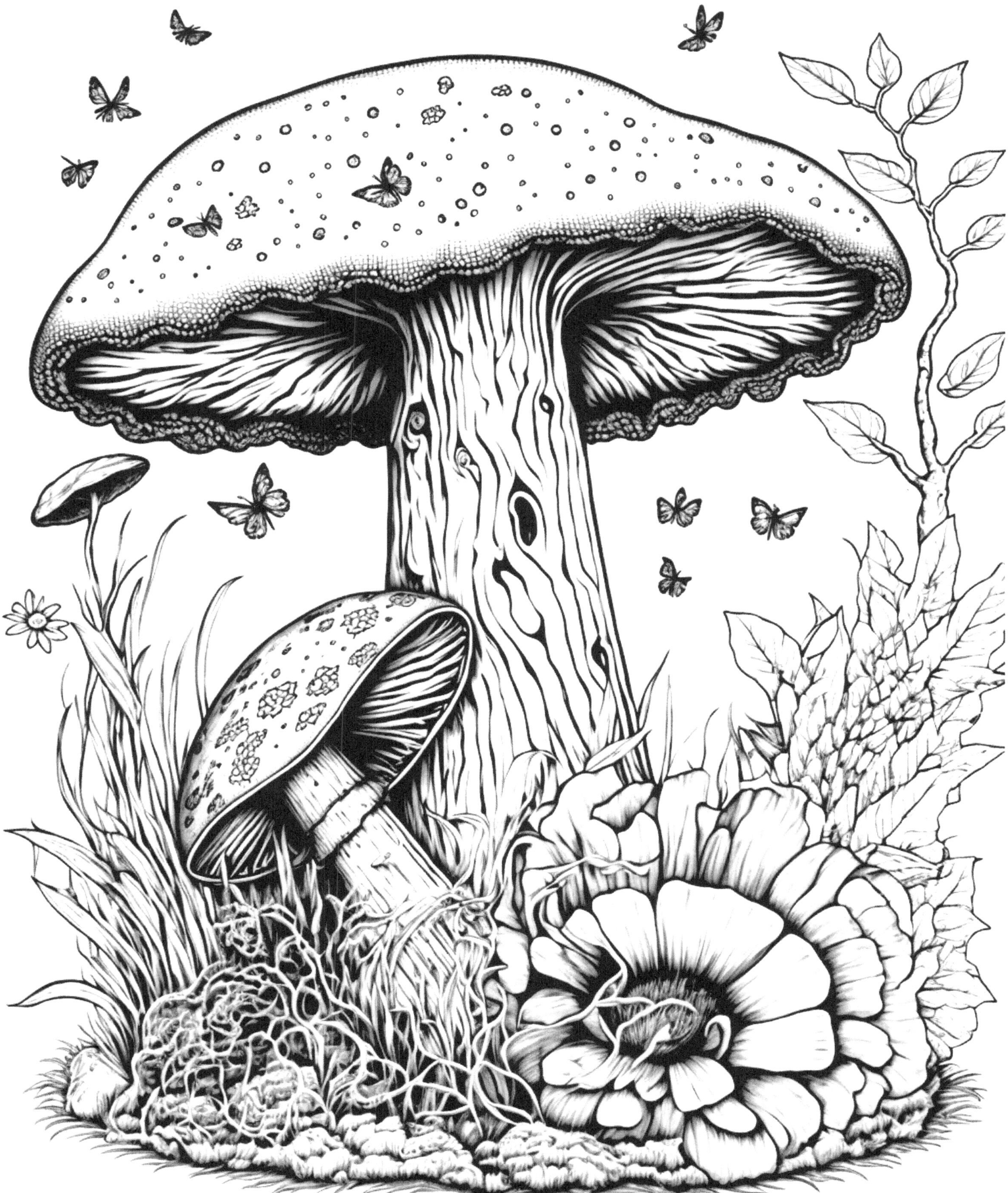

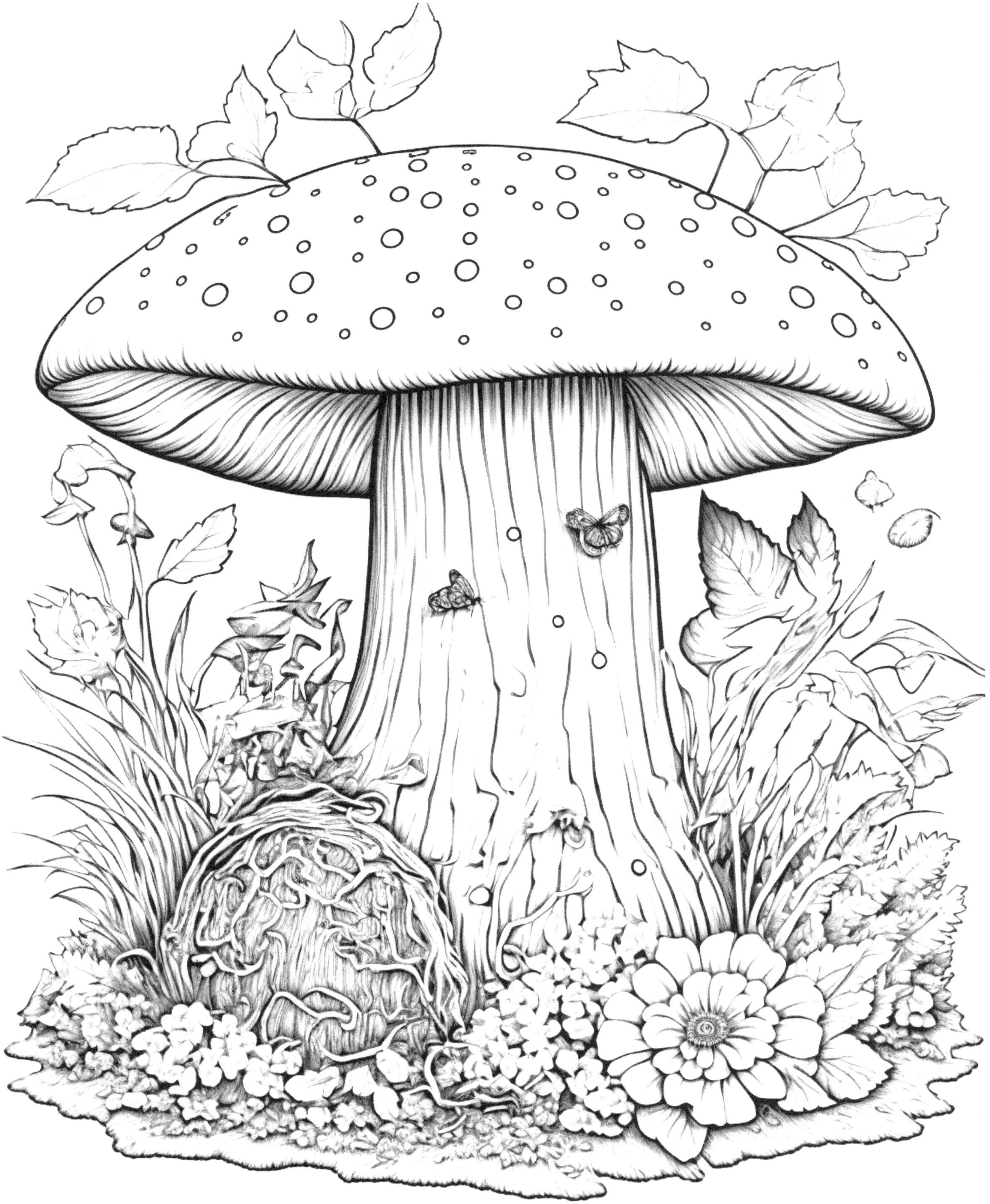

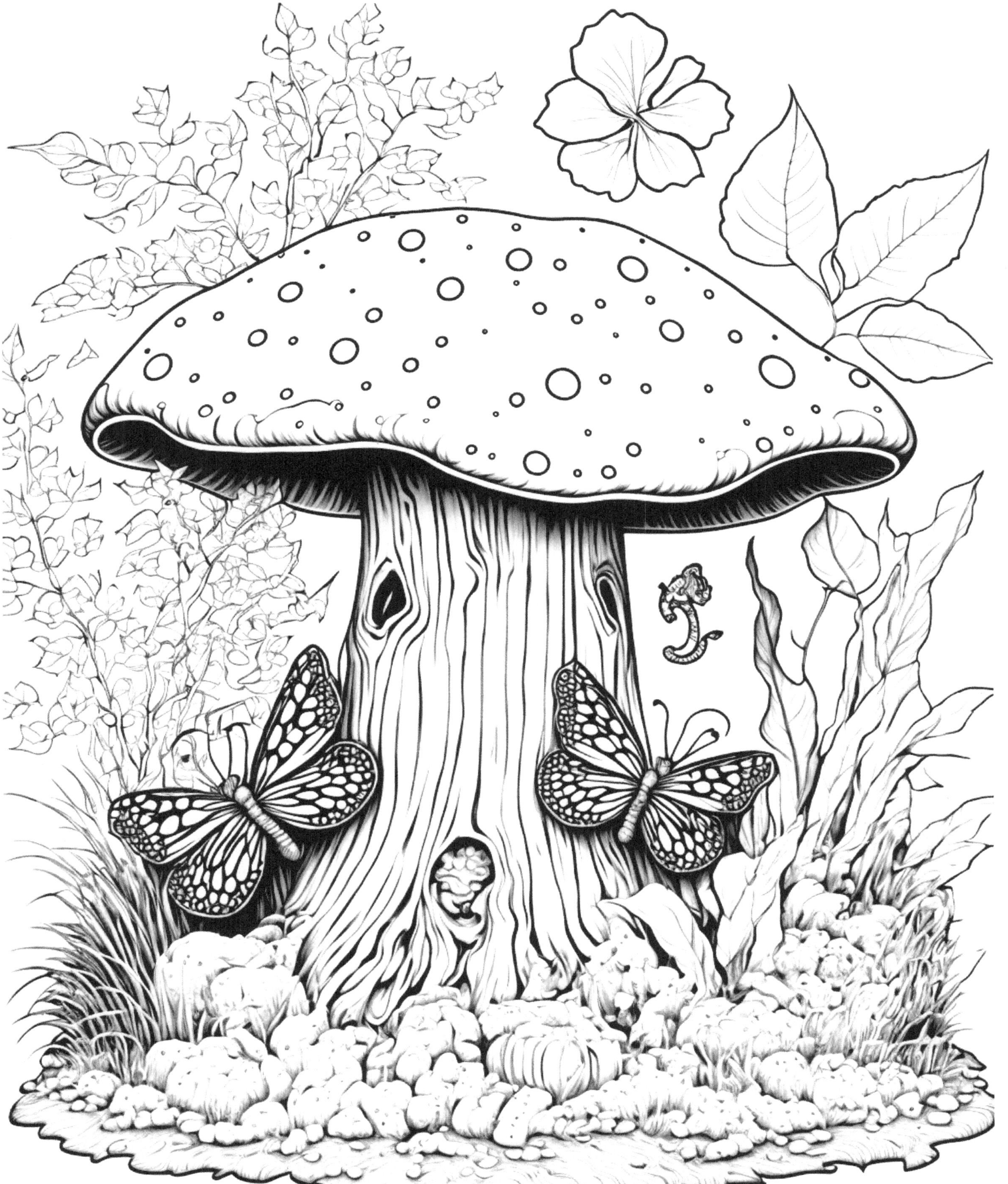

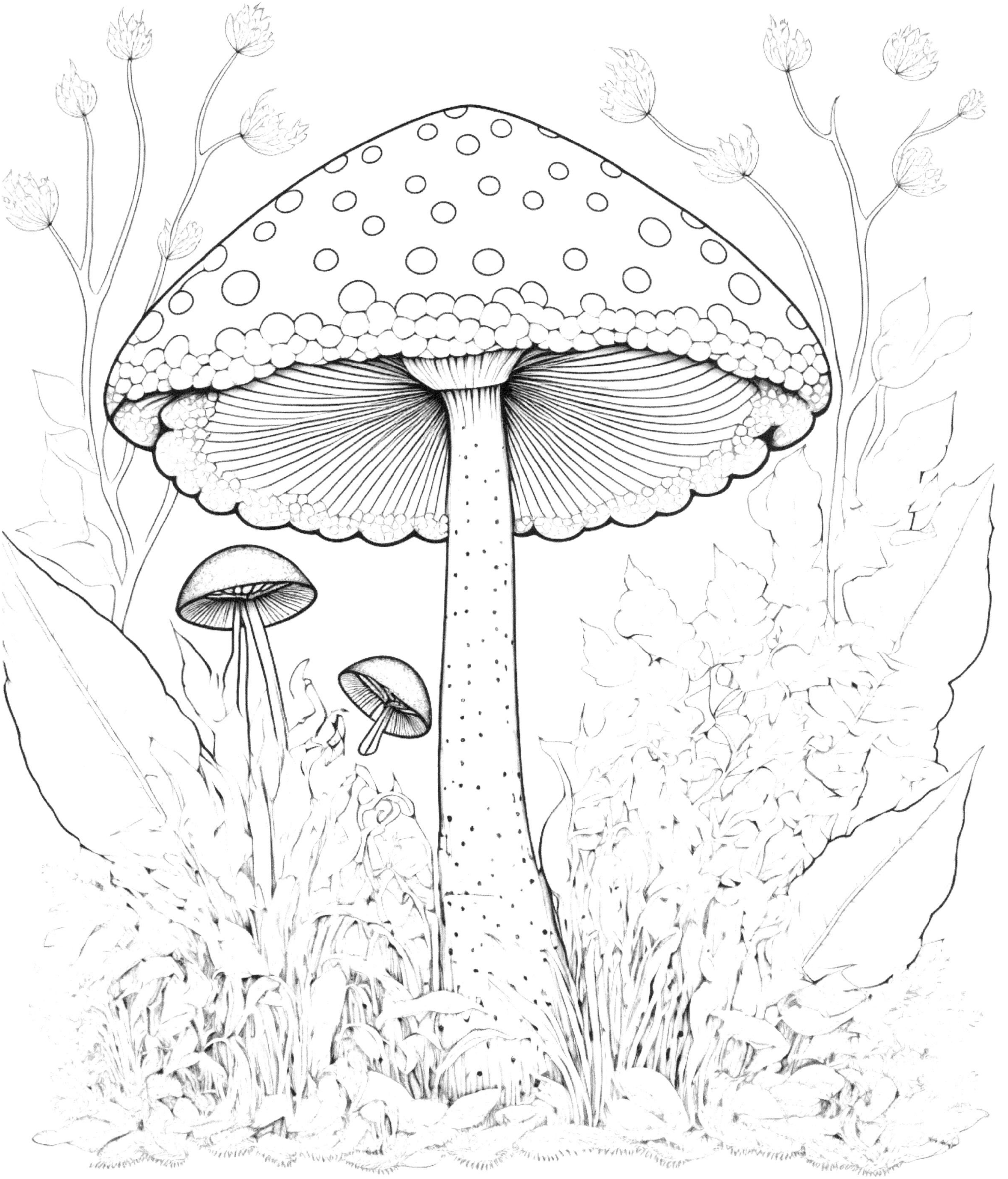

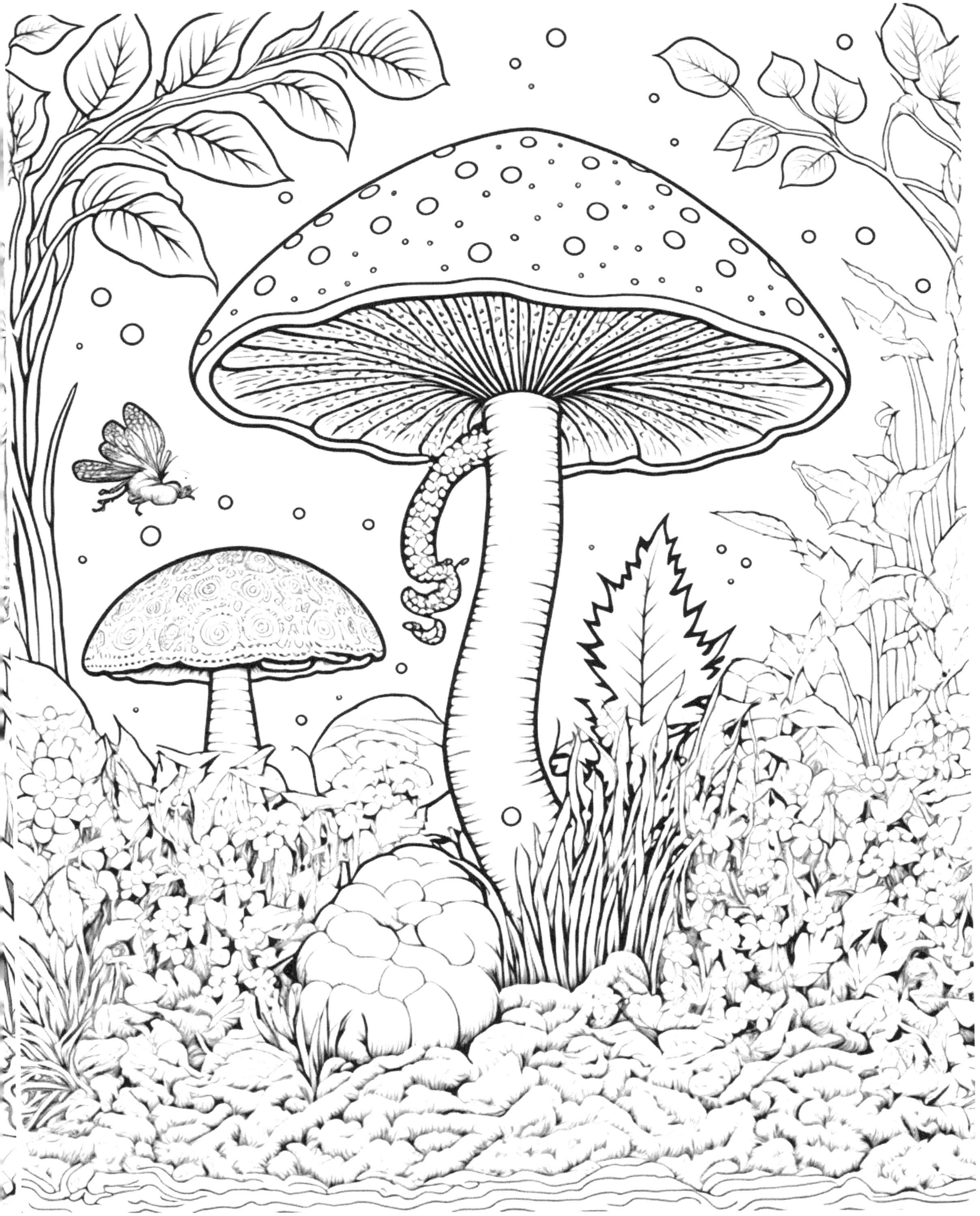

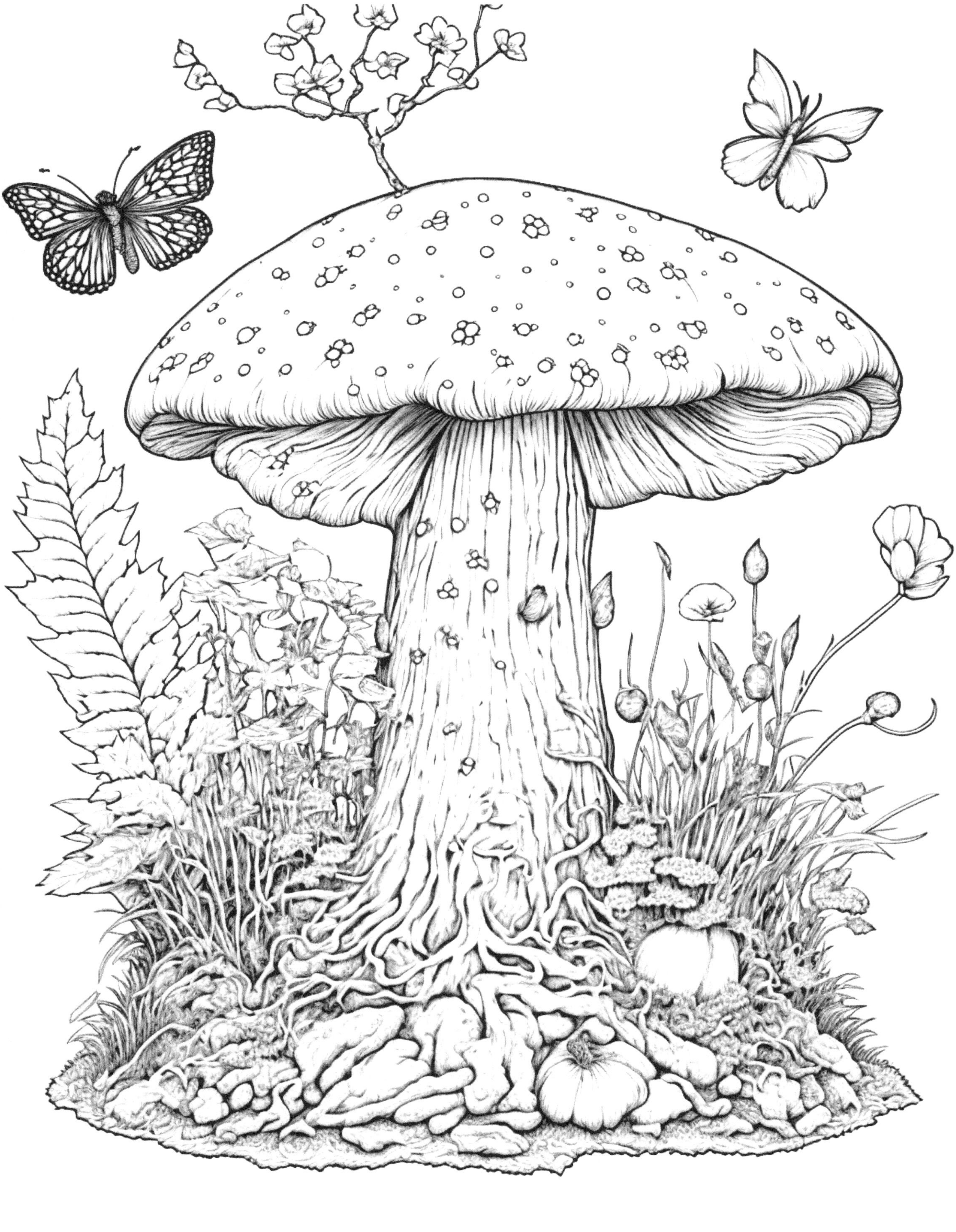

Made in the USA
Middletown, DE
19 May 2023

30901362R00057